HUMANISM

The Greek Ideal and Its Survival

WORLD PERSPECTIVES

Volumes already published

WORLD PERSPECTIVES · *Volume Twenty-four*

Planned and Edited by RUTH NANDA ANSHEN

HUMANISM
The Greek Ideal and Its Survival

BY MOSES HADAS

GLOUCESTER, MASS.

PETER SMITH

1972

Contents

World Perspectives

What This Series Means

It is the thesis of *World Perspectives* that man is in the process of developing a new consciousness which, in spite of his apparent spiritual and moral captivity, can eventually lift the human race above and beyond the fear, ignorance, and isolation which beset it today. It is to this nascent consciousness, to this concept of man born out of a universe perceived through a fresh vision of reality, that *World Perspectives* is dedicated.

Only those spiritual and intellectual leaders of our epoch who have a paternity in this extension of man's horizons are invited to participate in this Series: those who are aware of the truth that beyond the divisiveness among men there exists a primordial unitive power since we are all bound together by a common humanity more fundamental than any unity of dogma; those who recognize that the centrifugal force which has scattered and atomized mankind must be replaced by an integrating structure and process capable of bestowing meaning and purpose on existence; those who realize that science itself, when not inhibited by the limitations of its own methodology, when chastened and humbled, commits man to an indeterminate range of yet undreamed consequences that may flow from it.

This Series endeavors to point to a reality of which scientific theory has revealed only one aspect. It is the commitment to this reality that lends universal intent to a scientist's most original and solitary thought. By acknowledging this frankly we shall restore science to the great family of human aspirations by which men hope to fulfill themselves in the world community as thinking and sentient beings. For our problem is to discover a principle of differentiation and yet relationship lucid enough to justify and to purify scientific, philosophic and all other knowledge, both discursive and intuitive, by accepting their interdependence. This is the crisis in consciousness made articulate through the crisis in science. This is the new awakening.

Each volume presents the thought and belief of its author and points to the way in which religion, philosophy, art, science, economics, politics and history may constitute that form of human activity which takes the fullest and most precise account of variousness, possibility, complexity and difficulty. Thus *World Perspectives* endeavors to define that ecumenical power of the mind and heart which enables man through his mysterious greatness to re-create his life.

This Series is committed to a re-examination of all those sides of human endeavor which the specialist was taught to believe he could safely leave aside. It interprets present and past events impinging on human life in our growing World Age and envisages what man may yet attain when summoned by an unbending inner necessity to the quest of what is most exalted in him. Its purpose is to offer new vistas in terms of world and human development while refusing to betray the intimate correlation between universality and individuality, dynamics and form, freedom and destiny. Each author deals with the increasing realization that spirit and nature are not separate and apart; that intuition and reason must regain their importance as the means of perceiving and fusing inner being with outer reality.

World Perspectives endeavors to show that the conception of wholeness, unity, organism is a higher and more concrete conception than that of matter and energy. Thus an enlarged meaning of life, of biology, not as it is revealed in the test tube of the laboratory but as it is experienced within the organism of life itself, is attempted in this Series. For the principle of life consists in the tension which connects spirit with the realm of matter. The element of life is dominant in the very texture of nature, thus rendering life, biology, a trans-empirical science. The laws of life have their origin beyond their mere physical manifestations and compel us to consider their spiritual source. In fact, the widening of the conceptual framework has not only served to restore order within the respective branches of knowledge, but has also disclosed analogies in man's position regarding the analysis and synthesis of experience in apparently separated domains of knowledge suggesting the possibility of an ever more embracing objective description of the meaning of life.

Knowledge, it is shown in these books, no longer consists in a manipulation of man and nature as opposite forces, nor in the reduction of data to mere statistical order, but is a means of liberating mankind from the destructive power of fear, pointing the way toward the goal of the rehabilitation of the human will and the rebirth of faith and confidence in the human person. The works published also endeavor to reveal that the cry for patterns, systems and authorities is growing less insistent as the desire grows stronger in both East and West for the recovery of a dignity, integrity and self-realization which are the inalienable rights of man who may now guide change by means of conscious purpose in the light of rational experience.

Other vital questions explored relate to problems of international understanding as well as to problems dealing with prejudice and the resultant tensions and antagonisms. The growing perception and responsibility of our World Age point to the new reality that the individual person and the collective person supplement and integrate each other; that the thrall of totalitarianism of both left and right has been shaken in the universal desire to recapture the authority of truth and human totality. Mankind can finally place its trust not in a proletarian authoritarianism, not in a secularized humanism, both of which have betrayed the spiritual property right of history, but in a sacramental brotherhood and in the unity of knowledge. This new consciousness has created a widening of human horizons beyond every parochialism, and a revolution in human thought comparable to the basic assumption, among the ancient Greeks, of the sovereignty of reason; corresponding to the great effulgence of the moral conscience articulated by the Hebrew prophets; analogous to the fundamental assertions of Christianity; or to the beginning of a new scientific era, the era of the science of dynamics, the experimental foundations of which were laid by Galileo in the Renaissance.

An important effort of this Series is to re-examine the contradictory meanings and applications which are given today to such terms as democracy, freedom, justice, love, peace, brotherhood and God. The purpose of such inquiries is to clear the way for the foundation of a genuine *world* history not in terms of nation or race or culture but in terms of man in relation to God, to himself, his fellow man and the universe, that reach beyond immediate self-interest. For the meaning of the World Age consists in respecting man's hopes and dreams which lead to a deeper understanding of the basic values of all peoples.

World Perspectives is planned to gain insight into the meaning of man, who not only is determined by history but who also determines history. History is to be understood as concerned not only with the life of man on this planet but as including also such cosmic influences as interpenetrate our human world. This generation is discovering that history does not conform to the social optimism of modern civilization and that the organization of human communities and the establishment of freedom and peace are not only intellectual achievements but spiritual and moral achievements as well, demanding a cherishing of the wholeness of human personality, the "unmediated wholeness of feeling and thought," and constituting a never-ending challenge to man, emerging from the abyss of meaninglessness and suffering, to be renewed and replenished in the totality of his life.

Justice itself, which has been "in a state of pilgrimage and crucifixion" and now is being slowly liberated from the grip of social and political demonologies in the East as well as in the West, begins to question its own premises. The modern revolutionary movements which have challenged the sacred institutions of society by protecting social injustice in the name of social justice are examined and re-evaluated.

In the light of this, we have no choice but to admit that the *un*freedom against which freedom is measured must be retained with it, namely, that the aspect of truth out of which the night view appears to emerge, the darkness of our time, is as little abandonable as is man's subjective advance. Thus the two sources of man's consciousness are inseparable, not as dead but as living and complementary, an aspect of that "principle of complementarity" through which Niels Bohr has sought to unite the quantum and the wave, both of which constitute the very fabric of life's radiant energy.

There is in mankind today a counterforce to the sterility and danger of a quantitative, anonymous mass culture, a new, if sometimes imperfectible, spiritual sense of convergence toward world unity on the basis of the sacredness of each human person and respect for the plurality of cultures. There is a growing awareness that equality may not be evaluated in mere numerical terms but is proportionate and analogical in its reality. For when equality is equated with interchangeability, individuality is negated and the human person extinguished.

We stand at the brink of an age of a world in which human life presses forward to actualize new forms. The false separation of man and nature, of time and space, of freedom and security, is acknowledged and we are faced with a new vision of man in his organic unity and of history offering a richness and diversity of quality and majesty of scope hitherto unprecedented. In relating the accumulated wisdom of man's spirit to the new reality of the World Age, in articulating its thought and belief, *World Perspectives* seeks to encourage a renaissance of hope in society and of pride in man's decision as to what his destiny will be.

World Perspectives is committed to the recognition that all great changes are preceded by a vigorous intellectual re-evaluation and reorganization. Our authors are aware that the sin of *hubris* may be avoided by showing that the creative process itself is not a free activity if by free we mean arbitrary, or unrelated to cosmic law. For the creative process in the human mind, the developmental process in organic nature and the basic laws of the inorganic realm may be but varied expressions of a universal formative process. Thus *World Perspectives* hopes to show that although the present apocalyptic period is one of exceptional tensions, there is also at work an exceptional movement toward a compensating unity which refuses to violate the ultimate moral power at work in the universe, that very power upon which all human effort must at last depend. In this way we may come to understand that there exists an inherent independence of spiritual and mental growth which though conditioned by circumstances is never determined by circumstances. In this way the great plethora of human knowledge may be correlated with an insight into the nature of human nature by being attuned to the wide and deep range of human thought and human experience.

In spite of the infinite obligation of men and in spite of their finite power, in spite of the intransigence of nationalisms, and in spite of the homelessness of moral passions rendered ineffectual by the scientific outlook, beneath the apparent turmoil and upheaval of the present, and out of the transformations of this dynamic period with the unfolding of a world consciousness, the purpose of *World Perspectives* is to help quicken the "unshaken heart of well-rounded truth" and interpret the significant elements of the World

Age now taking shape out of the core of that undimmed continuity of the creative process which restores man to mankind while deepening and enhancing his communion with the universe.

RUTH NANDA ANSHEN

New York, 1960

HUMANISM

The Greek Ideal and Its Survival

I.

The Legacy and Its Distortions

FLUTED columns on public buildings, the technical vocabulary of philosophy and science, names like Antigone or Ulysses in titles of books and plays testify to a Greek ingredient in European civilization. How essential is this ingredient? Is it detachable, like architectural ornament on a steel-framed building, or merely economical, like nomenclature or terminology, or is it a functional element which supports the structure and determines its contours?

Those items in the Greek legacy which are most easily recognizable as such are in fact the least important. When we call an elderly sage Nestor or a lawgiver Solon, or when we adapt museum specimens for designs of buildings or costumes we are purposefully exploiting the exotic to achieve elegance. Borrowings are more significant in the degree that they are less easily recognizable. Works of literature which do not employ obviously Greek names and plots may be more profoundly influenced by the Greek than those which do, for the major genres and subject matter of literature, as of philosophy and plastic art, have been laid down by the Greeks. But the most significant influence of all is where the modern literary work or philosophic discourse is continuing an inquiry initiated by the Greeks, and with premises, objectives, and criteria of propriety established by the Greeks. Here the Greek ingredient is fundamental and continuously operative, and because it is so pervasive, because the amalgam is chemical rather than physical, it is harder to isolate and identify. But it is worth doing. The obviously exotic is an elegant subject for antiquarian study; the examination of the unconscious premises which govern relations between man and man, and man and external authority, which shape taste and which give direction to aspirations, may have more immediate relevance.

To pursue the examination with a mind free of contemporary or private preconceptions is extremely difficult, and the lenses which we must perforce use are bound to introduce distortions. Periodically, in past history, men have resorted to the classics afresh in order to find enlargement, and regularly what they found looks, in retrospect, like corroboration of their own particular programs. It is always doubtful, in each of the several classical revivals, whether the Greek was in fact seminal or even catalytic, or whether it was merely exploited to give authority and fullness to a movement which came into being independently. And the more doctrinaire and vocal the renaissance, the less substantial it was apt to prove.

Where the ancient paradigms have been most effective is in the matter of form, and even here the results have not always been wholesome. In the second century A.D., for example, there was a marked renaissance of classicism which scholars call the Second Sophistic. The movement was concerned exclusively with reviving modes of expression current in the fifth and fourth centuries B.C., and it avoided any concern with content so scrupulously that a critic who showed interest in matter as well as manner was condemned as a renegade. The modern reader is astonished to find de-

voted students of Thucydides and Demosthenes and Isocrates oblivious not only to their own world but also to
everything in these weighty authors except their forms of
discourse. Fronto, who was an intimate of the Emperor
Marcus Aurelius, was reputed to be the greatest literary
figure of his age, and the discovery of his correspondence
with the Emperor in a palimpsest during the last century
aroused the liveliest anticipations. But nothing more jejune
than his letters can be imagined. All that one remembers is a
note of reproach to the Emperor for turning from rhetoric
to philosophy. Two centuries later the Christian Ausonius
would reproach Paulinus more outspokenly for turning from
poetizing to a serious concern for Christianity.

There are other and clearer cases where preoccupation
with classicism has obstructed legitimate and desirable
progress. In the twelfth century Salerno was ruined as a
practical and flourishing school of medicine when its masters
became more concerned with the elegance of their texts than
with their proper business. The new interest in ancient texts
which characterizes the Renaissance of the Quattrocento
and Cinquecento did indeed promote liberation of spirit,
but the liberation did not spring new-fledged from texts
which happened to turn up. On the contrary, unfamiliar
texts were searched out because it was believed that these
would confirm and give direction to new ideas already
burgeoning. And when it reached its full flower the classicism of the Renaissance was as constricting as it was liberating. Jerome Vida (1490–1566), whom Alexander Pope
called immortal and ranked next to Vergil, wrote a most
influential *Art of Poetry* of which the sum and substance is
that every aspiring poet must model himself on Vergil, as

Vida himself did in his *Christiad*. The cult of Ciceronianism was so absolute that its followers would use no Latin expression not found in the works of Cicero; thus Pietro Bembo (1470–1547), who was cardinal and papal secretary to Leo X, would never speak of the Holy Ghost, and refers to the Virgin Mary only as *dea ipsa*.

From the point of view of literary art what the various renascences and Augustan ages learned from the classics was often based on misunderstanding or distortion, and is at any rate not what either the ancients themselves were most concerned with or what our own generation values most in their work. A case in point is the doctrine of the dramatic unities which the Renaissance derived from Aristotle's and Horace's treatises on poetics. The doctrine, at least in its canonical form, was based on misunderstanding and its rigid application amounted to distortion; and yet the ancient doctrine and models were responsible for the rich efflorescence of European drama. The important thing that the humanists learned from the ancients was that drama could be high art, mature and dignified and worthy of the best attention of the best minds, not a vulgar entertainment for a carnival mob. A Greek element was indeed operative, but to the profound and subtle probings of the human spirit which make Greek tragedy so meaningful to us the humanists appear to have been quite blind. And just as preoccupation with externals could dull discrimination of rich content, so it could of poor also. Except for the witness they bear to contemporary social and religious trends the Greek romances are negligible; but it was the example of the Greek romances which showed that prose fiction could be a systematic and artistic organization of a complex plot, and so ultimately made the novel possible.

For evaluating the ancients, even with respect to externals, the humanists abdicated completely to the critics of later antiquity. It seldom occurred to them to question an accolade bestowed by Cicero or Quintilian, or to seek excellence in writings to which these authorities were indifferent. The Quattrocento revered Homer, of whose text they were ignorant, because the Romans had praised him; and when their judgment had been sufficiently formed to prefer Vergil as the more sophisticated poet (as Vida emphatically does) they still accepted Homer's eminence as an article of faith. In the course of his own career Cicero turned from a preference for Herodotus to a preference for Thucydides because he identified himself with the Atticists, for whom preference for Thucydides was mandatory, and the Renaissance dutifully echoes Cicero's disparaging remarks on Herodotus. It is worth noting that official disapproval did not diminish Herodotus' popularity; the translation of Lorenzo Valla (1407–1457) was reprinted many times. For his edition of 1566 Henri Estienne provided a long preface in defense of Herodotus; but the object was apparently not so much to defend Herodotus as to criticize contemporary clerical deceptions. These, the preface indicates, are more numerous and more serious than Herodotus' deceptions.

In subsequent literary history, similarly, the classics, or particular passages or interpretations of them, served as a convenient stick to defend some current enthusiasm and belabor its opponents. The early nineteenth century, for example, saw a new and romantic attachment to the classics, but it is clear that the classics were not the seminal element but merely exploited, and frequently wrongly, to reinforce *Schwärmerei* independently arrived at. Shelley certainly thought that his Prometheus was a legitimate expansion, not a falsification, of Aeschylus': actually Shelley's rebel distorts Aeschylus as seriously as his torrential language does. Goethe was convinced that his *Iphigenie auf Tauris* was a perfect Greek tragedy, but a classical Greek audience would have been puzzled at the thought that an ardent barbarian king could learn self-abnegation from the mere presence of a virtuous Greek spinster. We need only compare the poses and costumes of nineteenth century and of classical Greek representational art to see why the Greeks were seized upon to symbolize release from all trammels; but, as we shall see, such idealization ignored other trammels which controlled Greek life.

It may be that our own assurance that we know the Greeks more truly rests upon a similar delusion and that we are merely finding in the Greeks more timely refractions of our own preoccupations. One may suspect that the currently fashionable approaches by way of folk-psychology and anthropology and new criticism are no more (if no less) valid than the allegorical interpretation of Homer practiced by the Stoics; but at least our quest for essentials is on solider ground because we attend more narrowly to substance than to form. The history of the interpretation of the Biblical book of Job affords an illuminating illustration. Theodore of Mopsuestia (died 428) excluded Job from his Bible because he believed that it was an imaginative, not a historical, work, whose author deliberately emulated the form and spirit of Greek tragedy. The Council of Constantinople of

553 restored Job to the canon, but its dramatic character continued to be recognized and commented upon. Theodore Beza, lecturing upon it in Geneva in 1587, divided it into acts and scenes, and Bishop Lowth in an extensive treatment of the book (1753) found that it fulfilled all the requirements of Aristotle's *Poetics,* except that it lacked action; it was therefore not a tragedy. But if the author of Job learned from Greek tragedy, as many contemporary critics hold he did, it is absurd to suppose that so consummate an artist and profound a thinker would feel himself bound by externals. The essence of the matter is that Job in his suffering, in his attitude to God (who is not, as he is elsewhere in the Old Testament, the patron of a particular nation), and in his acceptance is as like a tragic hero as he is unlike other personages in the Bible.

Modern adaptations of Greek tragedy in particular are essentially, not superficially, more faithful to their models than are those of Racine or Alfieri or Goethe. In the Greek the tragic figure must choose between sanctions each of which possesses recognized validity and the power to punish disobedience. In Aeschylus' *Suppliants* or in his *Oresteia* the alternatives can be schematized as Chthonic and Olympian. Adrastus must either deny the right of asylum to persons who have a familial claim upon it and thus incur the displeasure of the Chthonians, or expose his people to war with a powerful foreign enemy, which would violate Apollonian principles of orderly government; Orestes must either violate Apollonian principles of orderly government by failing to avenge his father's murder, or incur the penalties of the Chthonian Furies for slaying his mother. Revealed religion allows for no such alternatives; there is no parallel external authority which might sanction disobedience to the sole authority. In more sophisticated Greek thought, as in Euripides, the alternatives might be labelled *physis* and *nomos,* nature and convention, what a man owes to himself and what he owes to the community. When a contemporary playwright represents his modernized Greeks as torn between the claims of their own psyche and of society, he is expressing in rational language what the Greeks expressed in the language of myth. But did the modern learn about Ego and Id from the Greeks, or did he find among the Greeks convenient exemplifications of new knowledge otherwise acquired?

The danger of resorting to the Greeks for inspiration or corroboration in any doctrinal position is that preoccupation with one aspect must necessarily obscure rival positions which may indeed have enjoyed wider currency and exerted deeper influence. The most striking example is the persistent but essentially romantic view of the Greeks as uniformly rationalist, impatient and even contemptuous of the supernatural, concerned only with the intellectual and suspicious of the emotional. Now it is true that uncompromising intellectuality does in fact characterize much of the best Greek work, and true too that some Greeks were rationalist and impatient of the supernatural, and it may well be that rationalism and intellectualism, regardless of their influence in Greece itself, have been the most fruitful elements in the Greek legacy. But we must be aware that rationalism was never the sole nor even the dominant outlook in Greece itself, and that later ages which insisted that it was were only seeking buttresses for their own outlook. In the second century A.D. Lucian, who was a Syrian by birth, purposefully surrounds himself with what he fancies was the intellectual climate of the fifth century B.C. He writes, and very competently, not the contemporary idiom but the language of Plato; he disparages contemporary historians and philosophers by a comparison, usually tacit, with the masters of the classical period; but most of all he is scornful of irrational religious movements, in the assumption that such aberrations were alien to the great age.

But modern writers have accepted and propagated an equally romantic view of the classical period. In this conviction the eminent Rohde could speak of Plato with his dualism as "an alien drop in the Greek blood-stream"—as if any characterization of the Greeks which must exclude Plato could have validity. Now it is true that late and dubious authorities speak of Plato's journeying to the east, where he might have sat at the feet of native sages. But these stories derive from newly Hellenized peoples who were eager to claim cultural priority over the Greeks and one after another insisted that Plato himself had adopted their traditions. Actually there is no credible evidence that Plato made these journeys; what is more important, there is nothing in Plato's teaching which cannot be derived, by perceptible stages, from antecedent Greek doctrine. An author like Thucydides is justly admired for his critical and scientific approach and for his thoroughgoing rationalism; but Thucydides' own pages show how the Hellas of Hellas could be thrown into a delirium by the mutilation of the hermae and the violation of the Mysteries and how a leading statesman and general like Nicias could seal the doom of Athens by refusing to save her fleet because the moon was in eclipse. Thucydides does not say that military operations always started with a religious ceremonial because he assumed his readers would not need to be told. Such phenomena have always been known to have existed in Greece, but romantics have been reluctant to recognize their extent and pervasiveness. Now E. R. Dodds' *The Greeks and the Irrational* makes it abundantly clear that the Greeks were as continuously and deeply concerned with the supernatural as any people in history.

The distortion involved in exaggerating the rationalism of the Greeks brings other distortions in its train. It is frequently assumed, for example, that the Greeks viewed the organization of society as a human achievement, dictated by expediency and accommodated to emergent needs. On the basis of the pre-Socratic physicists, of the Hippocratics, and of the Sophists it is correct to say that such a view was held. Thucydides, who learned from the Hippocratics, represents society as having developed from savagery to civilization. The Epicureans in particular were concerned to propagate this view, and it is set forth in detail in Lucretius' poem *On the Nature of Things,* which is based on Epicurean doctrine. But Hesiod, who was a school textbook (one is tempted to say Sunday-school textbook), was much more widely known and revered in the classical period than the philosophers, and Hesiod describes the fall of man from a state of bliss through the impertinent curiosity of a woman and the consequent degeneration of man through ages of gold, silver, bronze, and iron to our present wretched state.

On a different level, Sappho has been exalted as the exemplar of unashamed eroticism expressed in uninhibited lyricism and simultaneously leered at for her supposedly naughty relations with her girl pupils. Sappho's poetic eminence and purity are beyond question, but our view of her personality and of the social climate she reflects must be altered by the new realization that she was an important and revered figure in the Orphic cult and that her school was a seminary in both modern senses of the word. The unself-conscious nakedness of the Greeks, in fact and word, has charmed Byronic rebels against stifling primness, but it is as easy for Victorians to find proof-texts as it is for rebels. In Greek schools, as Aristophanes describes them in *The Clouds,* boys marched in line, primly draped, and when they arose carefully smoothed the sand they sat on to foil drooling lovers. Phaedra's nurse, in Euripides' *Hippolytus,* offers to procure female help if Phaedra's malady is of a sort that could not be decently spoken of to a male physician. And when, in *Iphigenia Among the Taurians,* Orestes tells his elder sister that the story of their mother is not suitable for a maiden's ears, she says at once, "I am silent."

Other illusions of an earlier age have been corrected by our fuller appreciation of economic and social factors. We are stirred by the democratic ideal of Athens as set forth in Pericles' Funeral Oration, but we are aware that the entire system rested upon the institution of slavery, that citizenship was rigidly exclusive, and that women were relegated to an inferior legal and social status. There are splendid examples of chivalry in Greek warfare but also horrifying cases of calculated *Schrecklichkeit.* Brutality and inequitable legal disabilities and even slavery are of course to be found in relatively recent periods in our own history, and perhaps the Greeks are to be admired for having attained a social level which it has taken the world so long to surpass. But whether the Greeks were somewhat better than ourselves or somewhat worse it is clear that they were enough like ourselves to be measured by the same gauge, and not so superior or indeed so different as to be outside humanity as we know it.

It is because Greeks were like other people we know that we must be aware of such oversimplifications as have been remarked upon in the foregoing pages. Oversimplification is always tempting to students bred to filing cabinets and library classifications, and indeed has its own usefulness. It is convenient to speak of "Greek" or "medieval" or "modern" outlooks even if we know that all three are to be found in each of the three periods, provided we bear clearly in mind the gauge, whether of mass or of other significance, which we are employing as a point of reference. Greece happens to be a most convenient laboratory specimen for the student of politics or war or religious beliefs partly because the Greeks were highly articulate and are remote enough to be approached without passion, but mainly because within so small a compass of space and span of time they illustrate so many of the outlooks mankind has known, and in perceptible and comprehensible degrees. In view of such variety no single classification can properly embrace the whole, yet it is possible and profitable to choose a single salient element which is markedly characteristic and which therefore may have affected the majority which did not consciously share it or may even have opposed it. It is just such a characteristic, easily distinguishable from the mass both in Greece and elsewhere, whose effects may have persisted and are discernible in subsequent history.

To isolate the salient characteristic should not be difficult. What the world has admired in the Greeks is the remarkably high level of their originality and achievements, and this high level premises a deeply held conviction of the importance of individual attainment. The goal of excellence, the means of achieving it, and (a very important matter) the approbation it is to receive are all determined by human judgment. The whole outlook, in other words, is anthropocentric: man is the measure of all things. This does not imply that there are no gods; there are, but they behave as it behooves gods to behave, and man must behave as behooves man to behave, which is to attain the excellence he is capable of. The important point is that the sphere of the human and the sphere of the divine are disparate. In the chapters to follow we shall glance at possible explanations of the genesis of the doctrine of man the measure, see its expression in Homer and in the principle of heroization, its premises in the tragic concept of life, its importance in the pre-Socratics and the teachings of the Sophists, its formulation in Epicureanism, and its transmission to the modern world. In itself the doctrine of man the measure was never the sole or even the dominant view either in the population at large or among its spokesmen; indeed a good part of the surviving literature is in express opposition to the doctrine. Nevertheless, the outlook of which the doctrine is perhaps too stark an expression does seem to have been pervasive in Greek life, and through its ultimate products, if not in itself, it has been Greece's chief legacy to Europe.

Though the doctrine was not formulated until the time of Protagoras, its implications are present in Homer, and from Homer the line proceeds, in the stages indicated, until the Roman period. Rome and Christianity diverted it, but it survived as a trickle and again burst into a torrent in the age of humanism. Again man was frankly recognized as the measure, and has continued to be until modern times. The humanists closed the loop in the line at the point where it had been diverted, and carried it forward. Other items in our Greek legacy are only trimmings or implications of the central doctrine of man the measure.

But if we insist that the Greeks were essentially like other peoples we are left with a puzzle. If the Greeks were of different clay their extraordinary cultural achievements and the anthropocentric doctrine upon which these are premised would require no special explanation; but how could a people so like ourselves have attained the heights it did so long ago and have imposed its own patterns upon Europe? To this question we must now address ourselves.

II.

Who Were the Greeks?

IF A stranger to our world should wish to understand the motive forces of European society, the premises and the objectives of our ways of life, he could learn most economically by studying the Greeks. He could learn from later societies also, of course, though perhaps less economically; he could not learn at all from antecedent societies. If this is so, and to the degree that it is so, it was the Greeks who determined the directions European civilization would take. Their effective means for doing so was not, as has been suggested, the periodic recall of their high achievements in disparate categories of arts and sciences, but an informing principle which subsumed and embraced the totality of the Greek phenomenon. Whatever this principle was, how did the Greeks come to formulate and follow it? How did a small population in a small country during a small span of time come to invent European civilization and in some fields carry it as far forward as it has ever advanced?

There was a time, three or four generations ago, when Greek primacy was accepted as self-evident. Just as religious history began with Abraham, secular history began with Homer, and there was nothing very remarkable about it, for both came, by divine ordinance, so soon after the beginning of time. But then the telescope was turned right, and caught millennia of civilized life stretching so far back that the ancient Hebrews and Greeks seem much nearer to this end of history than to its beginnings. We now know not only that Homer and Abraham had predecessors but we have good grounds for suspecting that these predecessors had something to do with each other. Why then the sudden efflorescence of Greek creativity, so fresh as to antiquate all that came before?

What particular chemistry precipitated this efflorescence must remain a mystery, but tentative explanations have been proposed. It has been suggested, plausibly enough, that the physical configuration of Greek lands shaped Greek character and political institutions. Because disparate communities are separated from one another by mountain ranges, the extremely particularistic and self-sufficient city-state came into being. Because the total community was small, a sense of individual importance was fostered and democracy was the natural consequence. Because the soil is thin and rocky, the business of getting a livelihood demanded strenuous exertion, which was then applied to other phases of life. It has been said also that the extraordinary clarity of the Greek atmosphere induced precision of observation and hence of conceptual reasoning also. And so on. All of this may be true, but the question then arises: Why did similar natural conditions in other parts of the world, and indeed in Greece itself at other conjunctures of time, not produce a similar efflorescence?

For the physical factors to operate, it must be that the composition of the people had to be right. Who then were the Greeks? For all their particularism and internecine rivalries, those we know were a homogeneous people. So much is clear from their language, in which differences from region to region are only dialectical, and from their religious institutions, which differ hardly more than their dialects. But this homogeneity appears to have been the product of a fusion of quite disparate strands. There was first a stratum of Aegean people, whether autochthonous or early immigrants we do not know, which had reached a very high level of material civilization, in certain centers, as early as the third millennium B.C. The Aegean people were overlaid by an invading race from the north, whom we may call Achaeans. Precisely when, we do not know. A short decade ago scholars doubted that it was much earlier than the twelfth century B.C.; since the Minoan Linear B was deciphered and discovered to be Greek we know that Greek was spoken in the Aegean, in mainland Greece as in Crete, as early as the fifteenth century. The decipherment of Linear B has enabled Cyrus Gordon to identify Linear A (of which the remains are not nearly so abundant) as a Semitic language. Thus, though the cultural affiliation of the pre-Achaean peoples of the Aegean is perhaps more complicated than had been supposed, the hypothesis of an Achaean invasion is confirmed and the Greek civilization we know is indeed the result of a fusion.

But the fusion seems to have been quite complete from an early period. Martin Nilsson has shown that the mythology of the Mycenean period, which is the mythology our classical literature presupposes, is already an amalgam of Aegean and Achaean elements so synthesized or harmonized or sublimated as to be indistinguishable to those who accepted the mythology. Homer, who is our earliest articulate witness, already represents the Greek ideal essentially as we know it from the classical period, and though ingen-

ious scholars find in the epic traces of the suppression of
earlier beliefs and practices—of Chthonic worship, for
example, with its occasional brutality and its matriarchal
organization of society—the victory of the Olympian and
masculine view appears to have been complete and the
reader senses no polemicizing in behalf of one outlook and
against another. But if Homer represents the dominance of
the Olympian view with its concomitants we must not suppose that the older view was extirpated, as is frequently the
case upon the advent of a new religion with claims to
exclusive truth. The presence in later literature of such
Chthonian elements as the Furies and human sacrifice (in
the case of Iphigenia at Aulis), things which Homer doubtless knew but chose to ignore, is evidence that the disparate
strands survived side by side in a mingled skein.

But the background of the Homeric epic is war, and
though it was composed centuries after the war it purports
to describe and even more centuries after the Achaean
invasions, its personages embody the ideals appropriate to
powerful and proud conquering chieftains. The traditions
which Homer used and expected his auditors to know were
surely very old; and if his picture of the heroic age is
idealized its value as testimony is unimpaired, for ideals may
be more potent than facts in shaping attitudes and directing
conduct. The Homeric ideal is summarized in a single line
—"To strive always for excellence and to surpass all others."
This is the principle of conduct which Hippolochus enjoined
upon his son Glaucus (*Iliad* 6.208) and Peleus upon his
son Achilles (11.784). The salient traits which Homer
ascribes to his personages—the enormous importance they

attach to individual attainment and reputation, their zeal-
ous sense of self-reliance, their ambivalent attitude to the
supernatural—are all expressions of this ideal, and precisely
the traits we should expect of a conquering warrior aristocracy; superimposed upon the traits of the autochthonous
peoples they fashion the ethos which was responsible for the
efflorescence of Greek civilization as we know it.

Now if it is true, to any considerable degree, that the
Greeks moulded the character of Europe, then Homer may
be Europe's most influential teacher, for it was Homer that
moulded the Greeks. This is no hyperbole. The Greeks made
the perpetuation of their peculiar ideals a matter of paramount importance and the chief object of their education,
and the principal vehicle for education was Homer. As far
back as we can feel our way we know that any Greek who
knew anything at all knew Homer by heart and that Homer
was consciously regarded as a guide to life. So persistent was
this reverence for Homer that when later ages found aspects
of his poems ethically objectionable they allegorized them
to conform to their own more sophisticated sensibilities;
they could no more reject the text than Philo of Alexandria,
who used allegorical exegesis for an analogous purpose,
could reject the text of the Bible. When, after the classical
period, Greeks were scattered all over the Near East, the
first thing any group did upon settling in a new place was
to establish a school where Homer was taught, and it was
the shared knowledge of Homer, in large part, which
enabled the Greek diaspora to retain a common spiritual
identity. And if it was the text of Homer which to any
considerable degree shaped and preserved or at least re-

flected the Greek ethos, we should be able to understand the Greek achievement better by considering the individual outlook, the attitudes to society, the relations to the divine, the objectives of life, which the Homeric epic might inculcate.

III.

The Heroic Code

THE MOST striking single feature of the Homeric ethos is the enormous importance attached to individual prowess, individual pride, individual reputation. Heroes of other epics prize their individuality also, but in none is the drive for self-assertion so ruthless and pride so paramount as in Homer. In Roman or Christian or Indian epic it is a function of heroism to submit individuality, however grandiose, to a higher sanction; the Homeric hero may not compromise loyalty to his own being with loyalty to any other, human or divine. The great model is Achilles, but the lesser figures are motivated by the same ideal, and their greatness can be measured by the nearness of their approach to Achilles. Achilles actually prays for the defeat of his own side in war, to enhance his own glory, and he allows his comrades to die in battle when it is in his power to protect them. By standards more familiar to us this is not merely reprehensible conduct but treasonable and punishable by death; in the *Iliad* it is accepted without question—Achilles would not be Achilles if he did not behave so. And when Achilles returns to battle it is still for a private reason, loyalty to his beloved Patroklos; if he had come to acknowledge the claim of loyalty to his side he should have seized the enemy king when he had him in his power and surrendered him to the authorities. His courtesy to Priam is only a more attractive manifestation of total concern with individuality. The lesser heroes differ only in degree. When, at a moment of weakness, a warrior is aroused, by human agency or divine, to bethink him of his courage, it is on the basis of duty to self, not obligation to authority or loyalty to the group, that the appeal is made. The only hero who behaves like a responsible officer in an army is Odysseus, and Odysseus' deftness in managing others is a personal expression of a different kind of prowess; Odysseus is already the *intellectual* hero which the *Odyssey* will reveal more fully.

But if an Achilles will refuse, in consideration of his individual pride, to assist his fellows by standing shoulder to shoulder with them in battle, he helps all men by being himself. He and others like him earn the title of hero because they enlarge mankind by demonstrating man's capacity for greatness, by endowing the commonplace things of life, food and weapons and clothing, with an aura of glory, by pushing back the boundaries of what is possible to man. "Hero" signifies not merely the principal character in a story but a man who by doing or suffering significantly, not necessarily with the motive of serving others, has enriched the lives of all. His superhuman stature is officially recognized, after his death, and he receives annual offerings on his particular day and his mediation is invoked in realms of activity appropriate to his heroism. No one can be a hero in isolation, without a community to enlarge, and no one is pronounced a hero until he is dead.

That is why tragedy, and in particular the tragedies of Sophocles, must involve the violent death of the principal personage. Sophocles' plays, indeed, often amount to a demonstration that a personage generally esteemed as a hero did in fact earn that high status. All are stark and uncompromising figures whose obsessive willfulness causes their deaths, but all are also useful to other men, who, if they desire the obverse of the coin, must accept with it its inseparable reverse. In each of the plays the chorus and the lesser characters advocate obedience to traditional and authorized usages, from which the generality of men must not deviate. But it is useful to see a strong man willing to deviate, at the cost of his life, for a significant cause.

Ajax is a brute, concerned only with his own reputation and indifferent to the plight of his self-effacing wife and dependent chorus; he is tender to his son Eurysaces only as an extension of himself. For the crimes which he has committed—attempted assassination of his commanders in time of war—Ajax richly deserves the denial of burial which the commanders decree. But upon the intervention of Odysseus, who speaks for the community, Ajax is in fact buried—which is tantamount to acknowledgment that his heroic status is recognized. We need Ajaxes, and cannot have them without the defects of their merits. And so with Heracles in the *Trachinian Women*. Softhearted critics see in his brutal command to his son Hyllus to marry Iole, who is the innocent cause of Dejanira's suicide, a recantation: not the erring husband of Dejanira but the youthful Hyllus is the proper mate for the youthful captive. Actually the command sets the seal on Heracles' brutality; he insists on holding fast to Iole in the only way left to him, through his son. But if we want a Heracles, as we do, we must accept a self-centered brute in the bargain. And so with Oedipus, whose intractable passion is not abated even when he is old and blind, but whose transfiguration, with the assurance that his grave will be for a blessing, is reverently set forth in the *Oedipus at Colonus*. And so particularly with Antigone. Creon is surely right in denying burial to the traitor Polyneices who would have destroyed his own city, and Antigone, who insists on burying him, is headstrong and insubordinate and a little in love with martyrdom. Ordinary people must not transgress the law as she had done, but ordinary people, as individuals, are enriched by the spectacle of a girl resolute enough to give her life for a cause.

In the sophistic enlightenment of which Euripides is a spokesman the legends of heroes may be criticized and sometimes the heroes themselves, but the institution of heroization is not. Indeed, Euripides often seems to be complaining that the legends obscured the real service of the hero and prevented it from being properly utilized. The searing experiences which earned certain notable figures their status would have been unnecessary but for unwholesome conventions, which a fuller understanding of the problem should serve to correct. If Athenian convention had not irrationally degraded women and foreigners and illegitimate offspring and indeed misconceived the meaning of heroism, the horrors of the *Medea* or the *Hippolytus* or the *Electra* (not all the figures concerned were surely heroes) need never have happened. But the epiphanies at the end of Euripides' plays which sometimes express his sharpest criticism frequently also provide an etiology for some established observance of a hero's cult.

Heroization was by no means limited to remote antiquity. Sophocles himself and a hundred other figures of the historical period attained heroism by significant doing or suffering which enriched the community. Anywhere a man found himself in Athens or the countryside it is unlikely that he was ever out of sight of some memorial to a hero. It was familiarity with the process of heroization that facilitated the practice of deifying kings of the hellenistic period. Deification was of course a more serious matter, if only because the king became a god during his lifetime whereas heroization was necessarily a posthumous honor. The step from one degree to the other was an easy one for a Greek community to take, however, to express gratitude for important royal favors received or hoped for.

More significant, from the cultural point of view, is the difference in psychology. Heroization premises outstanding and uninhibited individual attainment; deification of a king inhibits individual attainment. We move, in modern parlance, from free enterprise at its most individualistic to the organization man. An analogy with Egyptian usage is instructive. Egyptian dead were embalmed to preserve their bodies for the longest possible duration, and not only was a stone facsimile included in the tomb for the use of the dead in case the original deteriorated, but sometimes a spare head of stone was added in case the first facsimile should be damaged. The important difference is that these representations of the man were not for the benefit of the living but only of the dead, as their being sealed in the tomb makes amply clear. The Greek memorial was not for the use of the dead but of the living, as an example and an encouragement to emulation. That is why classical Greek portrait statues are not realistic but idealized. Men are not shown old or sick or troubled even if they were so when the statue was carved, but in their idealized prime, with individual blemishes glozed over.

The high importance attached to individuality and individual attainment and reputation in the Homeric age persisted into the classical period and beyond. The transition between the two, both with respect to chronology and with respect to the shift in objectives, may best be illustrated from the institution of agonistic festivals, which retained their high importance in Greek life from Homeric times to the end of antiquity. Our own familiarity with athletic competitions and championships makes the great festivals called Olympian, Pythian, Isthmian, and Nemean, where men foregathered from all over Greece to compete for high distinction, seem natural. It seems less natural that these festivals included competitions in music and poetry also. It seems even stranger, but perfectly consonant with the competitive spirit in Greece, that the Dionysiac festivals, at which somber tragedies were presented, were also in the form of agonistic contests, with first, second, and third prizes. But most significant of the extent of the competitive spirit is the fact that festivals for competition in dithyrambic poetry were celebrated apparently in every considerable community. We are told of Simonides (who composed the epigrams for the battle of Thermopylae) that he won fifty-six victories in dithyrambic contests. This he could not have done unless he won several prizes, at different localities, in single years.

The recognition of high achievement which was the object of these contests is essentially a continuation of the outlook which fostered heroization, and which must surely reflect if it does not create a climate in which the attainment of acknowledged excellence is a normal ambition of the individual. If expertness in any calling was not accorded high respect the minor arts of the Greeks would not show such flawless taste and humble potters would not take pains to sign their work. We should surmise pride in craftsmanship from the high degree of specialization which Plato posits; and the Funeral Oration of Pericles makes it a distinguishing mark of the Athenian democracy that excellence in any field is recognized and rewarded by public esteem. On the other hand, the Athenian polity never became a bureaucracy of professionals. Political equality was secured by the use of the lot for election to certain offices, but where special competence was required the system of sortition was qualified. In choosing judges for tragic competitions, for example, first, some weeks before the competition, very large panels of suitable persons were chosen and their names deposited in urns; then, when the plays were presented, the requisite number of names was drawn from the urns and the persons thus chosen became judges.

Without the insistence upon recognition of individual worth (such as would become second nature to a population bred on Homer) the Athenian democracy would have been impossible; and only democracy of the Athenian type, in turn, could foster the peculiar originality of the Athenian achievement. Under the leveling authoritarianism of Sparta, where males from six to sixty were continuously under military discipline, individual enterprise in any direction was impossible. Nor could it flourish under absolute monarchy, even where, as in Ptolemaic Egypt, the kings bestowed generous subsidies upon literature and learning. The Alexandrians wrote only to impress each other; there was no longer a homogeneous citizen body out of which they could rise by acknowledged ability and by whose continuing approval they could be sustained and spurred to yet higher achievement.

The obvious objection to deriving Athenian attitudes from Homer is that the epic represents a thoroughly aristocratic point of view, which has regularly been more hostile to democracy than kingship has been; in antiquity and later, king and people have often stood together against barons. But the objection is not fatal. Aristocratic the heroes of the epic certainly are, and their status is made clear by the circumstance that they are descended from gods. Not only they but their weapons and horses are often provided with impressive genealogies, and they fight not against an indiscriminate mob but only in single combat against their peers. The position of the epic heroes is indeed suggestive of medieval chivalry, and the motivation of the chivalric code is very precisely expressed in the famous colloquy between Sarpedon and Glaukos (*Iliad* 12.310 ff., translation of Richmond Lattimore):

> Glaukos, why is it you and I are honoured before others
> with pride of place, the choice meats and the filled wine
> cups
> in Lykia, and all men look on us as if we were immortals,
> and we are appointed a great piece of land by the banks
> of Xanthos,
> good land, orchard and vineyard, and ploughland for
> the planting of wheat?
> Therefore it is our duty in the forefront of the Lykians
> to take our stand, and bear our part of the blazing of
> battle,
> so that a man of the close-armoured Lykians may say to us:
> 'Indeed, these are no ignoble men who are lords of Lykia,

these kings of ours, who feed upon the fat sheep ap-
pointed
and drink the exquisite sweet wine, since indeed there
is strength
of valour in them, since they fight in the forefront of the
Lykians. . . .'
let us go on and win glory for ourselves, or yield it to
others.

But for all their pride of race and warlike prowess the
epic figures are not Germanic knights. They and the
audiences that delighted to hear their tale were concerned
also with the ordinary tasks of daily living. Similes repeatedly
invoke humble and workaday images—a stubborn ass, flies
about a milk pail in a farm steading, and the like. Royal
ladies wash clothes, not only in the fairyland of Phaeacia
but outside the gate of Troy. Achilles' divinely wrought
shield carries a scene of tilth being turned up by the plow,
and Odysseus himself can boast (*Odyssey* 18.365 ff.) of
his ability to plow a straight and deep furrow and to make
hay. In the Homeric world, it has been reckoned, communities could usually be numbered in three figures and but
rarely in four, and in groups so tiny prerogatives of blood
must be limited. Classical Athens was of course much larger,
but still a city-state in which each citizen must count for
something. When Gilbert and Sullivan sing of "The Aristocrat who banks with Coutts, The Aristocrat who hunts and
shoots, The Aristocrat who cleans the boots" they may
properly conclude that "When every one is somebodee Then
no one's any body." In Athens, as we shall presently hear
Pericles say, a man whose occupation was humble was still

expected to do his part in government and might achieve political prominence.

Childish minds identify themselves with the most incredible feats of romantic heroes, but where a work of almost canonical prestige presents heroes who do not transcend the limits of probability even adults identify themselves with them. So communities which lived by the Old Testament have considered themselves as continuators of the Old Testament modes and outlooks, and so the Greeks did with reference to Homer. This was possible and indeed inevitable because the Homeric heroes are credible and intelligible. At a great crisis, when a hero has spent spear and sword, a Homeric hero might lift a boulder so big that *"two* men such as live today" could hardly lift it. In Apollonius of Rhodes the ratio is changed to four, and in the *Aeneid* to twelve. As the ratio rises the ability of a reasonable adult to identify himself with the action diminishes. By training and special exertion we could at least approach two; twelve is too remote to be considered a possibility. Or in another area, when Glaukos exchanges his golden armor for Diomede's bronze, we approach the hyperbole of romance, but are quickly brought back to the realities of life (*Iliad* 6.234 ff.):

> But Zeus the son of Kronos stole away the wits of Glaukos
> who exchanged with Diomedes the Son of Tydeus armour
> of gold for bronze, for nine oxen's worth the worth of a
> hundred.

The most eloquent expression of the Athenian ideal is the Funeral Oration attributed to Pericles in the second book of Thucydides. In an oration for a patriotic observance a man is of course no more on his oath than he is in a funeral eulogy, but the important thing here is not the degree to which the oration represents the truth but the fact that Pericles or Thucydides thought that this was what the Athenians believed and liked to hear. The central part of the speech (2.37 ff.), with unimportant omissions, runs as follows:

Our form of government does not compete with the institutions of others. We do not copy our neighbours, but are an example to them. It is true that we are called a democracy, for the administration is in the hands of the many and not of the few. But while the law secures equal justice to all alike in their private disputes, the claim of excellence is also recognised; and when a citizen is in any way distinguished, he is preferred to the public service, not as a matter of privilege, but as the reward of merit. Neither is poverty a bar, but a man may benefit his country whatever be the obscurity of his condition. And we have not forgotten to provide many relaxations from toil; we have regular games and sacrifices throughout the year; at home the style of our life is refined; and the delight which we daily feel in all these things helps to banish melancholy. Because of the greatness of our city the fruits of the whole earth flow in upon us; so that we enjoy the goods of other countries as freely as of our own. Our city is thrown open to the world, and we never expel a foreigner or prevent him from seeing or learning anything of which the secret if revealed to an enemy might profit him. We rely not upon management or trickery, but upon our own hearts and hands. And in the matter of education, whereas they from early youth are always undergoing laborious exercises which are to make them brave, we live at ease, and yet are equally ready to face the perils which they face. We do not anticipate the pain, although, when the hour comes, we can be as brave as those who never allow themselves to rest; and thus too our city is equally admirable in peace and war. For we are lovers of the beautiful, yet with economy, and we cultivate the mind without loss of manliness. Wealth we employ, not for talk and ostentation, but when there is a real use for it. To avow poverty with us is no disgrace; the true disgrace is in doing nothing to avoid it. An Athenian citizen does not neglect the state because he takes care of his own household; and even those of us who are engaged in business have a very fair idea of politics. We alone regard a man who takes no interest in public affairs, not as a harmless, but as a useless character; and if few of us are originators, we are all sound judges of a policy. The great impediment to action is, in our opinion, not discussion, but the want of that knowledge which is gained by discussion preparatory to action. For we have a peculiar power of thinking before we act and of acting too, whereas other men are courageous from ignorance but hesitate upon reflection. We alone do good to our neighbours not upon a calculation of interest, but in the confidence of freedom and in a frank and fearless spirit. To sum up: I say that Athens is the school of Hellas, and that the individual Athenian in his own person seems to have the power of adapting himself to the most varied forms of actions with the utmost versatility and grace.

Point for point the significant elements in this inventory of Athenian character may be derived from the Homeric outlook. What gives force to the argument that preoccupation with Homer had something to do with its origin and perseverance is the circumstance that such an inventory could not be derived from any other literary work. And what galvanized the Athenians into restless striving for excellence in whatever came to their hands to do was the same charge that spurred Homeric heroes to their displays of prowess—"To strive always for excellence and to surpass all others."

To Americans who are bred to the cult of success and measure it by the frequency with which a Name appears in public print this code does not seem very remarkable, except possibly in the starkness of its formulation. But we must remember that in large areas of human society, and in the same area at other times, ambition of this kind cannot be taken for granted. The predecessors of the Greeks appear not to have had it, nor did their successors for a thousand years after the Greco-Roman civilization was submerged. Perhaps it is more than a coincidence that the striving for excellence flared up again (and continues to this day) concurrently with the renewed preoccupation with Greek literature and the outlooks that literature inculcated. The key to that outlook, both among the Greeks and among the humanists, is the doctrine of man the measure.

In the humanist age the assertion of the doctrine of man the measure involved tension with a contrary doctrine which had long held the field. An equilibrium of a kind was reached in what is called Christian humanism. But what kind of equilibrium did the Greeks reach? Ordinary Greek life too was permeated with religious institutions and observances; gods are named or their presence felt in almost every page of Greek literature. How then could the anthropocentric principle assert itself? To answer this question we must look at the nature of Greek religious beliefs and Greek attitudes toward the supernatural.

IV.

The Supernatural

DESPITE all that has been said in praise of their rational-ism the Greeks were as intensely and continuously concerned with proper attitudes to the supernatural as any people we know. This concern appears, in some degree, in every book the Greeks wrote and in every statue they carved, and the greater the work, the more central the concern with the supernatural tends to be. In the course of the fourth and following centuries, it is true, art forms literary and plastic tend to lose the religious burden they were originally designed to serve and come to be cultivated only for their aesthetic value; but almost always the emptied form took on a new religious content. The *Argonautica* of Apollonius of Rhodes is mere belles-lettres, because it retains the epic form without epic seriousness, but then Vergil fills the form with a new and different religious meaning. Other forms exhibit an analogous progression.

If awareness of the supernatural was so central a preoccu-pation in the Greek intellectual climate, some understand-ing of its religious premises is essential for an appreciation of the Greek outlook in general. But understanding re-quires a great effort of the imagination. It is hard enough for a modern to naturalize himself into the intellectual climate of classical Greece; to make himself at home in its religious climate is almost impossible. The trouble is with the word "religion," which two millennia of the Judaeo-Christian tradition have encrusted with meanings now inseparable from it. Faith has little to do with it; even the militant atheist premises the familiar tradition for his opposition. And the difficulty is aggravated, not lessened, by the circumstance that for considerable areas, possibly because of common origins in the remote past, Greek and Hebrew premises and practices are very like one another; the problem would be less complicated if the two climates were wholly diverse.

Typical attitudes to Homer illustrate the difficulty. The supernatural element in the epic is impossible to ignore, as any unprejudiced reader must see, and yet in ages of enlightenment, ancient and modern, admirers of Greek rationalism did ignore it as an integral factor. One explanation of the gods is that they were merely poetic decoration, to enhance the importance of crucial scenes by making them require divine intervention or to clothe the whole, as a romantic poet might, with the dignity of archaism. A more plausible method of dealing with the divine (and other) crudities is to dismiss them as allegory: this method was practiced, by Theagenes of Rhegium, as early as the sixth century B.C., and was much elaborated by the Stoics. Now it may well be that when Athena prevents Achilles from attacking Agamemnon in the public assembly, an intended meaning is that Achilles experienced a sober second thought, or that Circe's transformation of Odysseus' crew indicates that excess of food and drink served by an enchanting woman may turn men into beasts. But no collateral meanings, however near the surface they may be and however valid, can supplant the plain meaning of language in a poet as direct as Homer. Actually allegorical interpretation, whether of the sixth century B.C. or of the nineteenth A.D., amounts to spiritual arrogance: the poet should and therefore probably did mean the thing the interpreter thinks appropriate.

But if we take what Homer says in its simple, not polysemous, significance, we encounter a confusion which must be disturbing to minds accustomed to theology systematic and consistent. Even when we have negotiated the leap from monotheism to polytheism the gods we see are disorderly and unpredictable and oscillate between extremes of kindliness and cruelty. Even on the question of the sovereignty of Zeus, where we should expect a definite and consistent position, there is ambiguity; sometimes Zeus is sovereign, bound by no will but his own, and sometimes he is subordinate to Fate and only the executive arm for the decrees of Fate. Here too, plausible explanations have been proffered. One is simple anachronism. A poet dealing, on the basis of tradition, with an intellectual environment which prevailed half a millennium before his own time would naturally and unwittingly introduce later concepts. There are apparently unwitting anachronisms in the armor, metals, social organization, and other usages which Homer attributes to his people: why not then in religion also? Another explanation is that the tradition which Homer followed was already an inconsistent conflation of disparate elements, corresponding to the different racial strains represented in Homer's dramatis personae. We emerge then with something like the documentary hypothesis as applied to Genesis; discrepancies are explained by R's faulty welding of J and E.

The analogy of Genesis is instructive. R himself and untold millions of his readers were unaware of inconcinnities but accepted Genesis as an integral entity corresponding to their apprehension of the relations between God and man. So Homer and untold numbers of his readers have been undisturbed by inconcinnities and have accepted the totality of the epic as an adequate and illuminating representation of the actual relations between gods and men. Nor need we condemn them as naïve for so doing. Aside from the circumstance that only brooding scholars closeted in their studies perceive the inconsistencies, it is only a sophisticated superstition which demands that the relations between man and the supernatural should be reducible to a unified system consistent and explicable at every point. The confusion presented by the phenomena of religious belief in Homer and later Greece does in fact represent the confusion of life, as I shall attempt to show more fully in subsequent paragraphs; and phenomena deriving from disparate sources survived side by side because each supplied answers to continuing needs and because in combination they supplied answers for more complex needs as they developed, for which neither element alone could suffice.

The brief characterization of the components of early Greek religion which we must now attempt is not intended as an antiquarian investigation of sources, therefore, but as a help toward discerning the actual operation of the elements, severally and in combination. Areas of uncertainty are so large that whatever can be said must be tentative, and since lines of demarcation are ambiguous, schematization is only an artificial device to facilitate description. In general we may recognize three strands, which may be designated Chthonic, Olympian, and Orphic. The sharpest distinction can be drawn between the Chthonic and Olympian, corresponding respectively to the indigenous and incoming elements of the population; but even here we must observe at once that Apollo, who is the perfect embodiment of the Olympian ideal, has been shown to have definite affiliations with the Near East. The Orphic movement, because of its salvationist traits, appears to have the closest affinities with what we commonly think of as eastern religion, though so far as we can see it was not an importation. We shall glance briefly at all three in turn, and first at the Chthonians.

The Chthonians seem to be connected with the widespread cult of the Great Mother, which has been thought to premise a matriarchal order of society, and are concerned with fertility in man and nature. They are logically feminine in nature and their psychology has been called feminine. Ties of blood are of the first importance, and the more exigent as the relationship is closer. Motivations for action are sentimental rather than rational. Relationships with persons are direct and immediate, not from a distance as with far-shooting Apollo or his sister Artemis. Punishment is meted out not by judicial inquiry but by a mechanical rule; bloodshed must be requited by equal bloodshed, without regard to extenuating circumstances and with no possibility for other compensation. The concern for blood carries with it notions of pollution; the taint is present and must be expiated whether or not a man is aware that he has infected himself.

The Olympians, by contrast, are masculine, remote, and rational. The principal figures are Zeus, Apollo, and

Athena, and Athena was born from Zeus's head without a mother and insists that her sympathies are always with the male. Because the Olympians were not monstrous in form but had the appearance and the emotions of handsome and well-bred men, they could be very close to their protégés. But immortality separated them from man by an unbridgeable chasm, and they could remind themselves, when they were tempted to interfere in the struggles of men, that it ill became their dignity to demean themselves on behalf of creatures of a day. Their typical effects they worked from a distance, whether by shooting arrows or putting thoughts in the minds of men. But most of all they operated by reason and eschewed sentimentality, and they were concerned for sane order in human society. But they never allowed concern for mortals to disturb their serene detachment. Certainly, and in this respect their difference from the deities of other peoples is most striking, their main function was not regulating and keeping book on the behavior of men.

Orphism, which premises a dualism of body and soul and enjoins progressive liberation of the soul from the shackles of the body, is most sympathetic to Europeans bred in the Judaeo-Christian tradition, quite possibly because through Plato and lesser channels it had contributed substantially to the shaping of that tradition. The development of Orphism is hard to trace with any exactness. The systematization of its cosmogony may be a later retrojection, as certain Neo-Pythagorean doctrines fathered upon Pythagoras demonstrably are, and a scholar of the standing of Wilamowitz could impatiently dismiss probings into Orphism as a waste of time. But direct references in Plato and allusions in Euripides and Aristophanes make it certain that the tradition of Orphism was very old, and it is clear that it influenced such diverse and influential teachers as Hesiod and Pindar, Pythagoras and Empedocles. Authors of the classical age, aside from Pindar and Plato, tended to despise Orphism, but it burgeoned into new life in the favorable atmosphere of the Hellenistic age. For a concise summary of Orphism we can do no better than quote from the article of Martin P. Nilsson, who is our best authority on Greek religion, in the Oxford Classical Dictionary: "Orphism implied legalism of ritual and life, mysticism of cult and doctrine, a speculative cosmogony and an anthropogony which emphasized the mixture of good and evil in human nature; it contributed to the transformation of the Underworld into a place of punishment. It made the individual, in his relationship to guilt and retribution, the center of its teaching. But its high ideas were mixed up with crude myths and base priests and charlatans misused them in practice." It is clear that Orphism had a considerable vogue in the pre-classical period, and if its origins were crude and orgiastic there is high probability that so choice a spirit as Sappho was officially connected with the cult. It is clear too that in its more refined and systematized form it flourished and influenced various mysteries in the Hellenistic age. Whether it had any considerable following in the bright light of classical Athens is problematical. Nevertheless, when we imagine the cool remoteness of the Olympians or the primitive starkness of the Chthonians we must think also of the Orphic cults which, if they did not provide a loving refuge in this world did ordain a discipline for spiritual awareness and did provide a tangible motive for spiritual aspiration.

A more instructive insight into characteristic Greek religious premises is accessible in the interactions between the Chthonian and Olympian deities as represented in literature. The ordinances of the Chthonians, being of the character of natural forces, were not expected to be rational; the rain falls alike on the fields of the righteous and the wicked. But when gods are imagined in the shape of sensitive humans, men expect that their ordinances shall be humanly intelligible. In monotheism the flaws in the universe become clamant and the problem of evil must eventually arise. In polytheism the individual deity need not embody ideals higher than human or indeed be accountable to human values of good and evil. And yet, as a being of human figure and capable of human emotions, his conduct must have some meaning comprehensible, and therefore somehow profitable, to his public.

In literature the clearest picture of the distinction between the Chthonians and Olympians is that presented by Aeschylus in the *Oresteia,* and in particular in the last play of the trilogy, the *Eumenides.* Apollo, in keeping with his concern for the rights of the male and for orderly government, has bidden Orestes to avenge the murder of Agamemnon, a king who was killed by a woman. By Apolline standards the fact that the woman was Orestes' own mother was indifferent; killing one's mother is no more or less heinous than killing any other elderly female. But by Chthonian standards the blood tie between mother and son is the closest possible, and matricide therefore the most heinous crime in the calendar. Orestes makes his difficult choice in favor of Apollo, and the Chthonian Erinyes, in keeping with their allotted function, proceed to persecute

him. The trial of Orestes, which will settle the issue between
the two views, takes place in a court newly established by
Athena, with Apollo arguing in defense. The Erinyes need
ask only one question: "Did you kill your mother?" When
Orestes must acknowledge that he did, the case is finished
in their sight. They are not interested in extenuating circumstances or in degrees of guilt; blood that has been shed,
for whatever reason, must be requited by blood shed in
turn. Apollo argues that the mother is not the true parent
of the child but only the nurse of the father's seed; this is in
effect a denial of the claim of blood, and of the matriarchal
principle with which it is involved. He maintains also that
the murder of a king is particularly evil, thus not only
emphasizing the Olympian concern with order, but also
denying the principle of automatic pollution by introducing
the factor of degrees of guilt. The Erinyes on their part are
convinced that it was the deterrents they represented that
maintained order in the world, and that if their function
were questioned chaos would ensue. The implications of
their eventual reconciliation we shall examine presently.
For the present we may note that the institution of a court
of law, where circumstances and degrees of guilt are examined and determined by a jury of the defendant's peers,
is a great stride forward in civilization. The mechanical law
of blood for blood with its corollaries of corporate and
hereditary guilt has been supplemented if not supplanted by
the rule of reason.

Other of Aeschylus' plays, notably the *Suppliants* and the
Prometheus, similarly turn upon an adjudication between
Chthonian and Olympian views. The *Prometheus* presents
a difficult philological problem. Not only is it different from

the other six extant plays of Aeschylus in form and language, but where the other six uniformly exalt Zeus almost to the level of omnipotence and omniscience of the God of the Old Testament, the *Prometheus* shows him as an unfeeling tyrant. Some scholars have found the discrepancy so striking as to deny the play Aeschylean authorship. But a great part of the difficulty may be that the theology of the *Prometheus* is higher rather than lower than the reader expects. Prometheus, who belongs to the Chthonic order, is a friend of man and alone made it possible for man to survive by supplying him with a series of crutches; being men, our own sympathies are naturally on Prometheus' side, and we can only look upon the grievous punishment Zeus inflicts upon him as senseless tyranny. But Zeus, who was indeed new to his office and admittedly had much to learn, had a completely different plan in mind; he operates, as it were, by a non-Euclidean geometry where we and Prometheus and Job's friends who are equally certain that wisdom will die with them, are limited to the Euclidean. Zeus's design had been, as Prometheus ruefully says (234 f.), "to bring the whole race of mortals to nothingness and to create another." In view of the wretched state in which Zeus found mankind, when only Prometheus' tinkering and pottering could keep them alive, this might have been an admirable plan, but it must take great imagination for a mortal to approve of it. Prometheus is without imagination and without rationality; he works only by sentimentality, which is the Chthonian way and wrong.

In the *Suppliants* the fifty daughters of Danaus who have fled marriage with their Egyptian cousins take a long while to convince King Pelasgus of Argos that they are in fact of

Argive descent (and so entitled to asylum by right of blood), and it is only when they have done so and threatened to pollute the land that the king cries out (438 ff.), "I am driven to this stark pass—a mighty war against one side or the other; there is no escape." The one side is the Chthonian, which will be outraged if people entitled to it are denied asylum; the other is the Olympian: to incur the danger of war with a powerful foreign enemy for a sentimental cause is bad because it is unreasonable. We do not know how the trilogy of which the *Suppliants* was part ended, but it is clear that the conduct of the Danaids was not completely justified, for their refusal to marry was not based on sufficient grounds. They did marry their cousins, according to legend, and forty-nine of the fifty murdered them on their wedding night. These are the Danaids in Hades, eternally busy with the futile task of carrying water in a sieve.

The ambivalent ending of the *Eumenides* is clearer and more germane to our purpose. When the jury voted half for acquitting Orestes and half for condemning him, Athena herself, by the rules of procedure which she had previously laid down, broke the tie by voting for acquittal. The decision, then, amounted to something like "innocent, but don't do it again." Even manifest murder does not automatically carry blood guilt. But what happened to the Erinyes is more interesting. With firm kindness Athena reconciles them to the new order by assigning them a new role; their former responsibility would now be otherwise discharged, but they remained earth deities, and as such their new function would be to bring blessings to the earth. Heretofore the Erinyes ("Furies") had been called Eumenides ("Kindly minded ones") only as a euphemism; now it has become their proper name. Even when new and better ways are introduced the old and familiar are not abolished but sublimated to new usefulness in an altered role.

It is here that we observe a significant difference between the religious outlook of the Greeks and that of the religions with which we are more familiar. When Judaism prevails in Palestine the older forms are made anathema (though their survival is attested by prophetic admonitions against backsliding), and upon the advent of Christianity both its Jewish and pagan antecedents are rejected. Monotheism is by nature exclusive and hence cannot tolerate rivals. Polytheism can, and it is the peculiarity of the Greek religion that several strands could continue side by side even when one had been partially discredited. Even where a belief is exclusive and codified, honest communicants sometimes find emotional attachment to different premises hard to overcome. Men who believe that the righteous dead enter into a blessed immortality should in logic be pleased when dear ones of whose righteousness they are convinced die, but in fact they lament. Reactions to the supernatural are not only complex but often contradictory, without the individual's being aware of the contradictions. The disparity which we find in the Chthonian and Olympian elements in Greek religion did not trouble the Greeks.

We return to Homer. In the light of what has been said, what is remarkable about him is not his confusion but his consistency. It is Homer who presents the Olympians most fully and most attractively, and it is the Homeric view of the motives and proclivities of the Olympians that fixed their character in subsequent Greek literature. If, as would surely seem the case, such tension between the Olympians and Chthonians as is reflected in the plays of Aeschylus already existed in the time of Homer, then Homer's neglect of the Chthonians would appear to be purposeful and his advocacy of the Olympians might make him one of the small handful of religious teachers who have affected the direction of civilization.

To assign such high importance to Homer does indeed seem to be allowing fancy too free a rein: when we know that the materials and forms of the epic are traditional, so that the very existence of Homer could be questioned and his contributions minimized, and when there is so little material for reconstructing the intellectual milieu aside from what the poems themselves provide, how can anyone presume to say that they contain significant theological innovations which can be attributed to Homer? And yet competent students have insisted that the Olympian religion, as it is reflected in later writers and therefore as it has affected European thought, is the creation of Homer, and it is worth our while to follow the train of their argument.

First, of course, we must agree that Homer is not only an individual creator but one endowed with extraordinary insights and originality. This recent trends in criticism have made it easy to do. The materials and techniques which Homer used are indeed traditional, but only a supremely gifted creator could have moulded them into the consistent artistic unity we read and have made of it so profound a commentary on the tragedy and glory of man. But how can we know with any degree of precision where Homer's own contributions, and particularly those relating to religion, are to be found? The only way is to examine what Homer has included in relation to the larger mass he must have known and to discern some directing principle which determined inclusion or omission or distribution of emphasis. Just such a procedure enables us to see that focusing the broader story upon the tragedy of Achilles is the work of Homer. From the point of view of religious attitudes it is noticeable that later accounts of persons and events associated with the tale of Troy reflect a more primitive outlook than Homer's, that they envisage such horrors as human sacrifice (as in the story of Iphigenia at Aulis) and cannibalism on the part of the gods (as in the story of Tantalus and Pelops). Whether there was a cultural backsliding after a higher level had been attained, or whether, as is more likely, the gains were now so secure that the older order could be looked at objectively, it is clear that Homer's omission of these horrors is intentional. It must be intentional too that he omits all mention of the earth deities (Demeter occurs only as a decorative epithet applied to grain); more striking, in the circumstances of the story, is the absence of any consideration of ritual pollution or infection by blood, or any thought of corporate or hereditary or indeed of any mechanical guilt. Emphasis on one factor and disregard of the other suggests that rivalry between the two was a live issue and that concentration on the Olympians was part of a considered program.

Part of the program, at least so much as had to do with suppression of matriarchy in favor of masculine dominance, had doubtless been set on foot long before Homer. Originally Helen may have been a vegetation goddess, like Persephone, which explains why she figures in a ravishment by Theseus as well as Paris; but Homer doubtless already knew her as a creature of flesh and blood. Penelope's suitors are indeed attracted by her charms, but what they chiefly desire is the prerogatives they will acquire by being consorts of the queen. In the case of Arete, who is described as a gifted diplomat, we can almost see the transition. When she suggests that her nobles give Odysseus gifts, an elder speaks up at once to say that the thought is excellent, but that the order should be given not by Arete but by Alcinous. But to discredit antiquated aspects of the old order was not enough. It was necessary not only for the Olympians to be given the upper hand but to be raised in stature and made acceptable and useful to civilized men.

The essential characteristic of the Olympians in Homer is that they are at once so near to men and so far. In shape, in family organization, in appetites, in capacities and interests they are like men. Their superiority, in respect to their likeness to men, is in degree. They are much handsomer, more elegant, more competent in their various specialties; but no more than men can they interfere with the laws of nature. They are not omniscient or omnipotent (as must be the case in polytheism), and they cannot, for example, keep a man alive when he is fated to die. Because of this nearness, men can meet them on their own level and sometimes become their protégés. But while men can look up to them as models or even aspire to surpass them in some accomplishment, they can never bestow on them the affectionate trust one bestows on a father or elder brother or strive for any kind of mystic union with them.

The one great distinction of the gods is that they are immortal, and this separates them from men by a wider and deeper chasm than if they were beings of a totally different order. Likeness only serves to sharpen the essential difference. Because they are deathless and ageless the gods' calculations are utterly unlike men's, with the result that they seem to men to be capricious and heartless. But since these gods did not create men or the world, they have no special responsibility to keep men happy nor indeed to see that the universe is without flaw. They do intervene in human crises, not, however, by introducing miraculous help from without but rather by helping a man suddenly attain the height of his physical and mental potentiality for some extraordinary effect, as by an electric charge. To say that the man lifts himself by his bootstraps is misleading, because it makes the intervention look like a poetic figure. The intervention is real; the gods' mode of intervention is by inducing (not importing) effects.

Typically, in Homer, the deity appears to an individual and disappears again of a sudden, and the poet makes a point of observing that he was seen by no one except the person to whom he appeared. Communication is on a human level. Athena's eyes may blaze out when she admonishes Achilles to put his sword back into its scabbard, but she does seize him by his hair and she does talk rationally, and when she reminds weary Diomede of his father's great reputation she is not in the least motherly but leans, like an equal, on the yoke of his chariot. In these and in other cases the effect of the epiphany is not to endow the mortal with supernal strength but to bring the capacities within him to their highest and sharpest pitch. Where no high capacities are present the goddess is not interested. An instructive intervention is the deception of Hector at his last stand against Achilles; the goddess makes him think he has a helper when he has not, and many readers find her conduct treacherous. Actually the deception is a grace. Hector was doomed and no god could avert his death; what Athena did enabled him to preserve his honor, by being killed fighting instead of running away. And the heroes know what the gods may and may not do; when they pray they ask for no such miracle as reversing the processes of nature but only for enhancement of their own potentialities.

As conceived by Homer, then, the Olympians do provide the enlargement of humanity which comes from appreciation of the divine, and high achievement and the reverse take on special meaning. But there is no outside power to wheedle or blame, and no refuge to console failure. Excellence, which must always be man's goal, is not precisely codified or graded: the conception is therefore fluid enough to accommodate itself to man's own rising standards and to situations and pursuits other than war. The universe may have flaws but they have nothing to do with theology. It is not that the gods lack sovereignty to suppress the authors of evil; the evil is not their concern but inherent in the nature of the world, like gravity.

What we have, in effect, is a world of gods and men in which each party attends to its own business and according to its own standards. That is why, though the gods of the epic are potent, the poem is still anthropocentric. It would not communicate to its readers the vicarious experience of high human prowess and high human drama if its personages were pawns in the hands of the gods or if they could dispose of superhuman resources to achieve their successes.

The measure of all things, as Protagoras was to say centuries later, is man; and just as Protagoras refused to speculate about the gods because in the nature of the case he could know nothing sure about them, so did the mortals in Homer also. That the gods are powerful is beyond question, and a prudent man will beware of crossing them, as a prudent man will step out of the way if a boulder comes crashing down a cliff in his direction. Why the boulder should behave so is an extraneous question and essentially irrelevant to his outlook on life. Critics sometimes speak of the gods in Homer as a kind of conspiracy to thwart man's happiness, and the view would have some cogency if the Homeric gods conformed to our opinion of what gods should be. The Homeric heroes did not think in terms of hostile gods. They knew well enough, as all adults know, that life is difficult and uninterrupted happiness virtually impossible; but they knew too that this is the nature of man, as sparks fly upward, just as it is the nature of gods to be forever as they are.

This view, implicit in Homer despite certain texts which might be cited to refute it, is explicit in Sophocles, who is the most Homeric of the tragic poets and whom the Greeks themselves acclaimed for his piety. Aeschylus, as we noticed, does appear to seek a moral justification for the ways of the gods: Sophocles is only convinced of their power and leaves their justice wholly out of consideration. Apollo's oracles do, beyond all human calculation, come to fulfillment, but to justify them on grounds of human concepts of equity makes nonsense. Attempts have indeed been made, from Aristotle onward, to justify the horrible things that happen to tragic figures by the doctrine of *hamartia* or the tragic flaw. But to say that Oedipus' bad temper was to blame for his punishment or Philoctetes' misstep for his is morally shocking; surely the punishment is monstrously disproportionate to the crime. It is as if we should say that a man deserved to be electrocuted because he disregarded a "Don't touch" sign. But the man is electrocuted nevertheless though a slight twinge would seem to be punishment enough. The point is that we do not expect electric current to observe our moral standards. In the problem of their relationship to man, the electrical or the divine are a fixed datum on one side of the equation; what Sophocles and his audience are interested in is how the human side will react, and as we have observed in connection with heroization, the human personages are admirable precisely in the degree that their conduct is completely independent and self-willed.

Euripides, who reflects a more radical enlightenment, holds essentially the same view of the gods. He is sometimes critical of them or of stories told about them, but he is not, as was once the fashion to label him, a rationalist. Disapproval of the gods is not the same thing as disbelief; the *Hippolytus* and the *Bacchae* are sufficient evidence that Euripides acknowledged the irresistible power of the gods in their own domains. Where his rationalism comes in is in his implied counsel to avoid the maleficent potential of the gods by getting rid of conventions which lead to distorting the nature of man. In a subsequent chapter we shall see that Euripides followed the Sophists in making the distinction between Nature and Convention the basis of his ethic: conditions imposed by nature we must needs accept, but those imposed by convention may be shaken off. Euripides would doubtless say that the gods themselves belonged to the first category and misconceptions of their character to the second.

But it is in certain speeches in Thucydides, who mentions such matters only incidentally, that we can most plainly see the demarcation between the human and the divine in the minds of Athenians. When in the famous dialogue at the end of the fifth book the Melians argue that it would be expedient for the Athenians to allow them to continue neutral, they are cut short with the remark that the Athenians must be left to judge their own interests. The only argument left to the Melians is that the gods would disapprove of the Athenian intentions, whereupon the Athenians reply that they know it as a law of nature that men rule where they can—and surmise, though here they cannot know, that a similar natural law prevails among the gods. What the Athenians proceeded to do to the Melians was shocking to men like Thucydides and Euripides, but not because it was a violation of religious law. This explains how a population which could be reduced to a delirium of panic by the mutilation of the Hermae and the violation of the Mysteries could with clear conscience exercise brutal tyranny over unwilling subjects. The sanctions were disparate, and the rule was according to the nature of man; when the subjects became strong enough they would by the same natural law throw off their yoke and rule the Athenians in turn. No sentimentality and no emulation of a divine paradigm was in question. It was the Romans who first felt compelled to justify empire as a divine mission to carry the white man's burden. Pericles, who was scrupulously observant of the requirements of religion, put the difference between the sanctions succinctly in a phrase in his last speech (2.64): "What comes from the gods we must bear perforce (*anagkaiōs*), what comes from the enemy with manliness (*andreiōs*)."

As far as we know—and as far as the classical Greeks knew—it was Homer who first made this rule of conduct enunciated by Pericles a norm for Greek society; surely the authority of Homer helped perpetuate it as a norm. If by that norm man is not master of his fate he is in the fullest sense captain of his soul, with every incentive to steer it to the highest reaches of excellence. And if we look away from revealed religions whose doctrines make every individual, however humble, a special object of divine love and divine solicitude and do not limit happiness to the handsome and well-born and competent, the beliefs of the classical Greeks would seem admirably suited for the conditions and aspirations of the classical Greeks—and of other societies with analogous conditions and aspirations. But if we take a factual view of life as it is lived in this world we see that even the well-endowed and the successful are visited by unhappiness. We must now see how the Greeks conceived of and dealt with the unhappiness inevitable to life—in other words, what the tragic view of life implies.

V.

The Tragic View

TRAGEDY too is a word in which modern associations have obscured original meanings. In common usage the word is a synonym for disaster, and more precisely a disaster which causes anguish such as is conveyed by the tortured expressions on conventional carvings of tragic masks. For a proper if pedantic approach to the meaning of the word we might limit its application to the plays produced in the theater of Dionysus at Athens in the fifth century B.C. and use the adjective "tragic" only to describe the essential characteristics of those plays. The Greek plays do indeed frequently present disasters which cause anguish, but the disasters and the anguish must have a special quality.

In the first place the person affected must possess stature; a little man's troubles, no matter how harrowing, can be pitiful and regrettable but not tragic. To call Arthur Miller's *Death of a Salesman* tragic is therefore metaphor, unless we are willing to acknowledge that Willy Loman represents a twentieth-century Agamemnon. Next, and more important, the suffering must not be the kind of accident which modern contracts call "an act of God" but somehow related to the character involved and preferably a consequence of a defensible moral choice he has made. Ideally the choice which the tragic figure makes is between two sanctions each of which has validity, as in the Aeschylean plays discussed above. But whatever the choice, and however imprudent it may prove, it is a choice that a reasonably good man of stature might feel justified in making. The fact that reasonably motivated actions do result in disaster is the essential of the tragic view.

Since there is no authoritative revelation to classify good and evil, the dramatis personae cannot straightaway be recognized as heroes and villains. Indeed there are no villains in Greek tragedy; unless we see that even Aegisthus, who is Clytemnestra's paramour and her accomplice in the murder of Agamemnon, has a degree of justification we misread the play. If there are characters thoroughly evil they are not central to the drama but only part of the machinery to bring on the disaster. To present an issue between an acknowledged wrong and an acknowledged right, with right triumphing in the end, is not tragedy but melodrama. Strictly speaking there can be no Christian tragedy, for when right and wrong are clearly identified the upshot must be a moral tableau or impious.

Thirdly, the issue must have a certain magnitude. Even men of stature must constantly make choices, but most are inconsequential. Tragedy often concludes with death not because it is a rule that it must but because the issue of life and death for a man of stature has obvious magnitude. It is not individuals that tragedy is concerned with but large types which can serve as paradigms. That is why we are given to see the figures only frontally, so to speak, not in the round, why we are told nothing of their idiosyncrasies. All that we are told is what is necessary to make the story intelligible. As in all Greek art, there is interplay between the individual and the generic, with the weight of interest on the generic.

And finally, as a consequence of the preceding requirements, the tragedy must serve to educate, first the personage
involved, whom suffering ripens to wisdom, and through
that personage the community to whom the play is addressed. Because tragedy is not melodrama or tableau, what
is taught are not copybook maxims in favor of observing
moderation and eschewing excessive passion or even of sub-
mitting to the caprice of the gods. Rather is the lesson that
good men, and almost in the degree that their goodness is
operative, are as the world goes subject to the slings and
arrows, but master them by maintaining their own integrity.
The price may be death, but every reader feels that Ajax or
Antigone dead or Oedipus blinded is really the victor. In
despite of obstacles, then, some of which his own nature
induces, the tragic hero extorts meaning and beauty out of
life and by so doing exhibits life's potentialities to his audience. If men and gods were on a level this might amount to
a struggle in which the gods were defeated, and if the gods
possessed holiness in the Judaeo-Christian sense resistance
would be blasphemy. But gods and men, for the Greeks,
belong to separate orders of being; the gods' part is their
concern, and beyond men's questioning. Men's part is their
own to fashion, within limits set by circumstances outside
their control (including the gods) and it is for them to play
their part with all the excellence they can attain.

Because such doctrine must be realized by laborious
stages, with light now from one angle and now from another, it cannot be blurted out but must be gradually un-
folded and illuminated by the resources of poetry and music
and dance. It should be unnecessary to remark that Greek
tragedy is too rich and multifarious to be summarized in a

single attitude to life. But it does happen that the attitude here noticed—in a word, the recognition of the disparateness of the world of gods and the world of men and man's consequent freedom, despite divinely interposed obstructions, to achieve the excellence of which he is capable—underlies all the tragedies, and, more important, is the central characteristic which sets them apart from other dramatic expressions. It is this which impelled Matthew Arnold to say of Sophocles that he saw life steadily and saw it whole.

Not only does classical tragedy differ from other by its characteristic tragic view; that same view pervades all classical literature and similarly distinguishes it, if not so markedly, from subsequent literatures. It is remarkable evidence of Homer's priority in crystallizing and setting forth the Greek outlook, if not of influencing it, that the tragic view is so clearly expressed in his epic. The central theme in the *Iliad,* the thing that makes it different from a mere narrative of a segment of a war and the thing which has engaged the interest of all readers, in a word, the thing that Homer himself created, is the tragedy of Achilles. We are told of Achilles that he was actually confronted with alternatives, a secure and long but commonplace life, or a short and glorious one. He deliberately chose the latter, to his great cost and to the benefit of all the Greeks. But because he was the kind of man who would make such a choice he was outstandingly exposed to frustration; he had sacrificed ease for glory, and now Agamemnon's usurpation of his prize Briseis deprives him even of glory. Even the structure maintains the tragic pattern. Until the ninth book Achilles' sulking seems justifiable, for he had been affronted without sufficient cause; but after Agamemnon's embassy had

offered honorable apology and rich restitution Achilles'
persistence in his wrath becomes morally questionable—or
would for a lesser man than Achilles. Actually it is in the
ninth book where we most fully appreciate Achilles' high
excellence as a human being. Such a man may, indeed
should, shape his own course; the excellence of Achilles is
more valuable to humanity than an easy victory. His capac-
city for thoughtful reflection and his tenderness to Patroklos
make the starkness of his will more meaningful; and when
his self-motivated consideration for Patroklos (not a divine
behest) has caused Patroklos' death he returns to battle
knowing that his rage is inhuman. When, at this decisive
duel, Hector offers Achilles a compact for the honorable
treatment of the loser's body, Achilles answers that they can
no more enter into oaths than can man and lion.

But though his rage persists through days of systematic
abuse of Hector's body, he does finally win through to assert
his nobility by returning Hector's body to Priam, in what is
surely one of the high peaks of all literature. It is true that
Achilles has received divine encouragement for his mag-
nanimity, as Priam has received divine aid for his dangerous
journey through the Greek lines, but these divine inter-
ventions, as we have observed, take their effect in the individual's mustering of his own highest potentialities; the
deed is Achilles' own and Priam's. When the essential
Achilles recognizes the essential Priam he bids him sit, for
there is no profit in lamentation.

> Such is the way the gods spun life for unfortunate mortals,
> that we live in unhappiness, but the gods themselves have
> no sorrow.
>
> (*Iliad* 24.525 f., tr. Lattimore)

Why they have none and why they spin sorrows for mortals
it is irrelevant to inquire; the only sphere where man can
act is the human, and there he must act to the utmost of his
capacity, regardless of interference from the other sphere.
What matters to man is man.

Our and Achilles' foreknowledge of his death add poign-
ancy but are not essential for the tragedy: the achievement
and the assertion of high nobility is matter enough to lend
the dignity requisite to tragedy. Nor are Achilles' anguish or
his prospective fate pathetic; each of us would be proud to
be an Achilles, if we possessed the requisite endowment, or
to push what endowment we have to its extreme potential,
as Achilles did. The "choric" aspect of the tragic figure's
career is important; no man can be tragic, any more than
he can be heroic, in a vacuum. It is because being truly
tragic is a public career that we can speak of the tragic view
as shaping the Athenian outlook on life.

And the tragic concept did permeate the Athenian outlook. The simplest evidence that it did is the large place that
the dramatic festivals occupied in Athenian life; nine tragedies were presented at each festival, under official auspices
and to large audiences, and they must have reflected if they
did not shape general outlooks. In modern drama, which is
obsessed with personality, it may require an effort of the
imagination to apply the vicissitudes of an individual to the
history of a community; but the protagonists of Greek
tragedy were idealized into types, whose experience could be
transposed to the careers not only of individuals but of societies. So much is plain not only from the largeness of the
characterization, which ignored individual idiosyncrasies,
but from the stylized mode of presentation, which avoided

any touch of naturalism or realism. Costumes, verse dialogue, the solemn song and dance of the chorus, all served to raise the action from the particular to the general. Orestes, confronted with his ultimate choice between the two sanctions in the *Choephoroi,* is so depersonalized a symbol that we need to be reminded that he is actually flesh and blood, and Aeschylus (in a most un-Aeschylean passage) reminds us by having his old nurse tearfully recall that she had to wash his diapers—convincing proof of humanity.

The application of the tragedy of the individual to the community as a whole may well have been part of the poet's intention. In his *Oedipus at Thebes* (New Haven, 1957) Mr. Bernard Knox maintains that the protagonist is to be understood as a paradigm of Athens. "The character of Oedipus," he writes, "is the character of the Athenian people. . . . The resemblance between Oedipus and Athens is clearly and firmly enough established for the poet to speak of them as one and the same. . . . Oedipus *tyrannos* and the Athenian *tyrannis* are so closely associated in the poet's mind and language that he can attribute to Oedipus faults which are not to be found in the hero of the play but in the actions of the city of which he is a dramatic symbol."

Identification with the symbol was easy, for the community no less than for the individual, because history itself was so often conceived of as a tragedy. The historians, Herodotus and Thucydides alike, gave the events they recorded tragic meaning and even tragic form. The great event which started Athens on its glorious career and remained the proudest boast of its orators was the repulse of the Persian invasions, in 490 and decisively in 479. The Greek victory is dealt with poetically in the *Persians* of Aeschylus, presented within seven years of the event, and in the narrative of Herodotus' history, written a short generation later. It is significant that Herodotus no less than Aeschylus tells the story from the Persian point of view. It could not be otherwise if history is tragedy, because though the audience is Athenian the tragic actors and sufferers were the Persians.

In Aeschylus it is the Persian realm, rather than King Xerxes who represents it, that is the tragic hero. The campaign against Greece was indeed an enterprise too grandiose for mortal men, and in a sense the Greek victory was a divine instrument for subduing overweening pride. Aeschylus and Herodotus alike, in contrast, say, to Euripides and Thucydides, are uncommonly concerned with religious factors. But the theme of *koros-hybris-ate* ("excessive prosperity-outrageous conduct-doom") is a conventional pattern, exigent, to be sure, but not fundamental to the interpretation of the events. Actually, except for Xerxes' offensive deportment, the enterprise of the Persians, considering their history and resources, was politically feasible; and Themistocles, who was responsible for the Athenians' success, could be said to be divinely directed only in the sense that his own faculties were operating at their highest efficiency. The action on both sides proceeds according to human measure. Athenians and Persians severally did what was in their nature to do; the gods, satisfactorily this time from the Athenian point of view but tragically from the Persian, did what was theirs to do. No Athenian would have suggested that the Persians should not have done what they did, providing the problem of logistics was adequately provided for. Within the century they themselves undertook similar grandiose enterprises, against Egypt and Sicily, and with similarly disastrous results. No Athenian is reported to have beaten his breast and cried *mea culpa,* but only "our bad calculations." The Egyptian campaign was undertaken at the direction of Pericles, who was scrupulously observant of the requirements of religion. The Sicilian campaign was under the command of Nicias, who was so observant that he failed to save the Athenian armament when he might have done so only because the moon was in eclipse. The point is that when he attempted to dissuade the Athenians from undertaking the expedition in the first place it was only logistics he argued from, not religion. It might be objected, of course, that other imperial peoples have similarly ignored religious restraints; but all empires after the Athenian have felt constrained to justify their conquests on the grounds that they were liberating the oppressed or civilizing the barbarian or simply carrying out a divine mandate enjoined upon an elect. In holding their empire the Athenians were merely carrying out what they conceived to be a rule of nature.

Authors of the late fifth century who separate the divine and human spheres may have been touched by the sophistic leaven. Herodotus definitely was not; more clearly than any other he posits a divine providence to govern the world, and is at pains to emphasize the validity of oracles, dreams, and the like. It is of special significance, then, that Herodotus too, like Homer and the others, keeps the divine and human spheres apart. All of the participants in the Persian war are reasonably good men, behaving as reasonably good men might; none are villains. When for their own reasons (which Herodotus as a pious man attempts to justify) the gods interfere, the good man meets with tragedy; but there is no hint that the possibility of such tragedy should deter them from action. It was not unreasonable for Xerxes, being Xerxes, to attack Greece, not unreasonable for the Spartans to hesitate to defend Athens, quite reasonable for the Athenians to argue and act as they did. And when Herodotus analyzes the Greek resistance he concludes (7.139), "If then a man should now say that the Athenians were the saviors of Greece he would not exceed the truth." The Athenians, not the gods; when it is a question of astute planning and vigorous action, men are the captains of their souls.

But not masters of their fate, which periodically impinges on their astuteness and vigor and makes all of human life and human history tragic. War itself is an example. "No one is so foolish," Croesus says after his defeat, "as to prefer to peace war, in which, instead of sons burying their fathers fathers bury their sons. But the gods willed it so." The distinction could not be more clearly put. If the gods were motivated as reasonable human beings are, there would of course be no war. Why the gods willed it is no more our concern than why they willed gravity or electricity. But how men behave, vis-à-vis electricity or gravity or war is their own affair, and it is the part of the good man to behave as well as he can and attain the highest excellence that he is, as a man, capable of.

This view is not incidental in Herodotus but stated almost as a program in his opening pages. Croesus, with whom the hostilities actually begin, had two sons, one a deaf-mute and the other, named Atys, normal, and because he especially cherished Atys and had dreamt that he would be killed by

an iron weapon, he removed all weapons and arranged for
Atys to be married at once and spend an indoor life. Now
some of the king's subjects whose lands were being ravaged
by a wild boar petitioned the king for help, and Atys
cajoled his father to let him join the hunt, on the grounds
that a boar has no iron weapons. A Phrygian, significantly
named Adrastus, who had been driven from home for having accidentally killed his brother, had been given asylum
and quite literally new life by Croesus. This man Croesus
enjoined to see that Atys received no hurt in the hunt, but
in protecting Atys from the charge of the boar Adrastus
unwittingly killed the son of his benefactor. There are no
good men and bad in this story. Everyone showed good will
and prudence, and it might reasonably have been expected
that the whole would turn out well. It did not, because the
will of the gods impinged; but we cannot blame the gods,
who attend to their own business according to their own,
not human, principles.

Another and kindred aspect of the program is presented
in the story of Croesus' encounter with the Athenian Solon,
told in the paragraphs preceding the Adrastus story. When
Solon arrived in Croesus' realm, Croesus ordered that his
magnificent treasures be displayed to him and then asked
him who in his opinion was the happiest man he had seen.
Solon named first Tellus the Athenian and then Cleobis and
Biton, all of whom had had satisfactory lives but all of
whom had died. When Croesus remonstrated Solon said
that no man can be called happy until he is safely dead—a
sentiment which recurs in Herodotus' friend Sophocles. It
is necessary, at the opening of the history, to display the
contrasting characters of the participants, but Croesus is

still treated with respect, not contemned as a vulgar barbarian. The point is that Croesus' way is right for Croesus
as Solon's is for Greeks. This is made clear in the story
Herodotus tells of Darius (3.38): "Darius, after he had got
the kingdom, called into his presence certain Greeks who
were at hand, and asked what he should pay them to eat
the bodies of their fathers when they died. To which they
answered, that there was no sum that would tempt them to
do such a thing. He then sent for certain Indians, of the
race called Callatians, men who eat their fathers, and asked
them, while the Greeks stood by, what he should give them
to burn the bodies of their fathers at their decease. The
Indians exclaimed aloud, and bade him forbear such language. Such is men's custom." Where the gods guide humanity, not merely visit it with tragedy from their own alien
sphere, only one usage is correct and all others a violation
of religion.

The nearest we come to divine punishment appropriate to
transgression is in the case of *hybris,* which we noticed as a
factor in the *Persians* of Aeschylus and which is equally a
factor in Herodotus. But *hybris* is never specifically defined
so that its limits can be recognized; the same conduct may
entail *hybris* or not according to the status of the persons
involved, the circumstances, the moral climate. Basically
hybris is what it is improper for a man to do in the circumstances in which he does it, what should cause a man to feel
aidos (roughly "shame"); only, then, if a man ceases to
remain in his human sphere is he subject to punishment for
hybris.

It is interesting to see that the primitive and widely dif-
fused notion that flaunted prosperity excites the envy and

anger of the gods is given a rational and moral meaning in Herodotus and one in keeping with the principle of separation between humanity and divinity. The classic case of mechanical *hybris* is the story of Polycrates, tyrant of Samos, told in Herodotus 3. Polycrates was warned by a correspondent in Egypt that his prosperity had reached dangerous proportions, and as a prophylactic contrived a piece of misfortune for himself by losing a valuable ring at sea. Even this ring he was lucky enough to recover, in the entrails of a fine fish that had been brought to the royal kitchen. Soon thereafter Polycrates indeed came to a painful and degrading end. Underlying this and similar stories of the punishment of excessive prosperity is the assumption that gods and men are similarly motivated; men more than six feet tall or possessing more than a ton of gold must be cut down because the gods are only seven feet tall and have only a ton and a half of gold, and hence fear the competition.

But when Herodotus came to deal directly with Xerxes' planned expedition, in the seventh book, a new element is introduced. It is not because they fear competition that the gods strike the prosperous down—they themselves are a hundred feet tall and own a hundred tons of gold—but because they know that excessive prosperity is regularly attended by *hybris,* and it is sometimes more convenient to strike *hybris* down before it displays itself to the full. This is thoroughly in keeping with the principle of the separateness of the spheres, and in keeping too with the principle that the gods' visitations inflicted upon humans are not susceptible to human canons; by attempting "what is too big for man" Xerxes and his like exempt themselves from the laws by which humanity is bound and invite punishment to which men who remain within the human sphere are not subject.

Thucydides may be cynical concerning oracles and the uses to which organized religion is sometimes put, but it is not true to say of him, as is sometimes done, that he is opposed to religion. He knows that the best calculations he (or his hero Pericles) can make are subject to unpredictable and irrational disturbances by outside forces; so far as human foresight can avail, the prudent leader will reduce the scope of the unknown X for harm, but Thucydides knows that the X cannot be wholly eliminated. Constantly when prospects for future developments are canvassed the adverb "humanly" is a warning that other elements sometimes enter in. These no righteousness can obviate. In the defense which Pericles addresses to the Athenians when they are disheartened by the plague and angry with him, he affirms stoutly that his calculations were good, so good that Athens could rise above the catastrophe; he never hints that the catastrophe was retribution for delinquencies or offers any other explanation than that it was an irrational affliction sent by the gods. What the gods send, he says, must be borne of necessity; but men must not, looking over their shoulders to the gods, abate their vigilance or their vigor or their fortitude.

If the gods' sphere is consistent in its unpredictability, the human sphere is predictable because it is consistent. Otherwise it would be impossible to deduce general rules of political behavior, which is the object of Thucydides' book. That is why, like the tragic poets and unlike the Roman historians, Thucydides tends to make his personages into types and tells us only so much about them as will make the history intelligible. History may not repeat itself but people do, even such marked characters as Alcibiades or Cleon or Brasidas; unless people repeated themselves no generalization about history could hold. Thucydides gives us a thoroughly clinical account of the course of the plague and of the class revolution in Corcyra, not because he has any suggestion or any hope that such disasters may be prevented in the future—they cannot be because they belong to the unpredictable sphere of the gods—but in order that future generations may know what human conduct to expect in such visitations.

Athenian lads of the fifth century who learned their Homer by heart, and possibly because Athenian lads had always learned Homer by heart, could recognize that the premises of the Homeric world obtained in their world also; they had not to learn that the currencies of *Erewhon's* musical banks were not legal tender in the world of action nor practice agile vaulting between the two. The gods were there, and there were numerous beautiful temples and rituals to make their presence known and to provide assurance that the other of the world's necessary spheres was in order; gods might even assist a man to summon up his highest potential as a warrior or a poet or a lover, but the responsibility was his alone and the glory; and the glory was the fairest prize a man could attain.

VI.

Man the Measure

TO FOCUS attention on a single view of the relations between man and the divine, as has been done in the pages preceding, is to ignore other facets of the Greek religious experience, some of which may indeed be incompatible with the view presented and which doubtless outweighed that view in volume of observance and following. If from an antiquarian point of view such distortion is indefensible, it may not be if our concern is with the specifically Greek ingredient in European culture. For one thing, the view enlarged upon is peculiarly Greek, in the sense that it cannot easily be paralleled in other cultures, and for another there may well be a causal nexus between the conviction that the spheres of gods and men are disparate and the extraordinary cultural attainments of the Greeks. In any case it is only an external and sophisticated scrutiny that distinguishes the strands in a mingled skein; the communicant accepts the totality without being aware of inconcinnities. And even if the Olympian strand was adulterated by others it may still have availed to infect the whole with its own characteristic tint.

Homer, it has been suggested, may have purposely glorified the Olympian at the expense of other strands, and the enlightened fifth-century authors we have glanced at reflect the same view, whether by choice or the force of literary tradition. Where they do not consciously sublimate non-Olympian beliefs, as Aeschylus does, they reveal a certain contempt for them, as Euripides and Thucydides do. But there were powerful spokesmen for other views too, Empedocles and Pythagoras among the pre-Socratics, Hesiod and Pindar among the poets. Among these the evidence of Hesiod is most important. He lived in mainland Greece, not Ionia, not long after Homer, and he alone can dispute with Homer the title of being the Bible of the Greeks. Homer's ethic is refracted by the totality of his narrative or extrapolated in detail; Hesiod's is direct admonition and exhortation. Where Homer is quoted by later authors mainly for decoration or interpreted allegorically, Hesiod is quoted as a direct guide to conduct. And what is curiously significant for our purposes, where scholars can only divine relationships between Homer and the east, in Hesiod there are demonstrable parallels in cosmogony, theogony, anthropogony, and gnomic utterances.

Homer's world is washed in a haze of glory; Homer himself looks at this world along with his audience, from without, and his own personality never intrudes. Hesiod's world is grim and workaday, and he addresses his audience from within it, in the first person, and speaks freely of himself. His father had been driven by poverty from Aeolian Cyme and had settled in Ascra, a Boeotian village near Helicon which was "bad in winter, wretched in summer, good at no time" (*Works and Days* 640). He himself was a shepherd and while he was tending lambs under Mount Helicon the Muses had taught him song. "We know how to speak many false things as though they were true," they had told him, "but we know, when we will, to utter true things."

This amounts to a program. Homer had said false things and Hesiod would say true. Homer had made it appear admirable for a powerful individual to take what he wished from weaker men; Hesiod is critical of folk-devouring princes who bend the law to suit themselves. He has a new vocabulary of epithets of approval and disapproval: truthful, never-lying, oath-keeping, law-abiding, righteous, unjust, sinful. It is even more significant that attributes which are complimentary in Homer—proud, strong-spirited, having prowess in arms—take on a pejorative sense in Hesiod. A people educated only in Homer would not be nearly so ready to accept Christian ethics as one informed by Hesiod.

Parallels with Christianity go further. We have the fall of man from a state of bliss through the curiosity of a woman. Before the fall man could provide for himself abundantly for a whole year with a single day's work, but now the gods keep the means of life hidden from man. Man has degenerated from a golden age through the ages of silver, bronze, and heroes, to the present wretched iron age. And things will be yet worse. Might will be right, and Aidos and Nemesis will depart from the world; there will be no help against evil.

Might does not make right for men; people who rely on their own strength do not realize how much greater the half is than the whole. For fishes and beasts and winged fowl Zeus has ordained that they should devour one another, for right is not in them, but to mankind he gave right, which proves the best. Zeus has thrice ten thousand spirits who roam, clothed in mist, all over the earth, and keep watch on judgments and wrong-doing of mortal men; Zeus' daughter

Justice tells him of men's wickedness and he ordains punishment.

Often even a whole city suffers for a bad man who sins and devises presumptuous deeds, and the Son of Cronos lays great trouble upon the people, famine and plague together, so that the men perish away, and their women do not bear children, and their houses become few, through the contriving of Olympian Zeus.

What is of interest here is the notion of communal guilt, the whole city being made responsible for the transgression of an individual, and the limitation of the punishment to this world. As in the pre-exilic portions of the Old Testament, a man's house may be cut off, but it is not envisaged that he will himself be punished in another existence. On the other hand, there is prospect that the good will be rewarded; at least the heroes of the Trojan and Theban wars enjoy bliss:

They live untouched by sorrow in the islands of the blessed along the shore of deep-swirling Ocean, happy heroes for whom the grain-giving earth bears honey-sweet fruit flourishing thrice a year, far from the deathless gods, and Cronos rules over them; for the father of men and gods released him from his bonds.

Zeus's virtual sovereignty (Hesiod uses "Zeus" and "the gods" interchangeably) and his concern for justice bring him nearer Old Testament than Homeric concepts. The glorification of Zeus with which *Works and Days* starts reads like a Psalm:

For easily he makes strong, and easily he brings the strong man low; easily he humbles the proud and raises the obscure, and

easily he straightens the crooked and blasts the proud—Zeus
who thunders aloft and has his dwelling most high.

This is a different world from Homer's, but though man's
conduct is more narrowly prescribed and observed he must
still strive for the excellence appropriate to him. Free enterprise is the heart of Hesiod's code. Competition which leads
to war is bad, but there is competition which is wholesome,
between potter and potter, builder and builder, beggar and
beggar, singer and singer. It is good for neighbor to compete
with neighbor in pursuit of wealth, and it is good to enjoy
the respect of your fellow man because your barn is full. But
wealth must be earned by strenuous work, not seized. Long
and steep is the path that leads to goodness, and it is rough
at the first; but when a man has reached the top then it is
easy though it was hard before.

Pindar moves in a world of aristocratic brilliance which
is at the opposite pole from Hesiod's. The gorgeous aura of
purple and gold through which he sees his noble figures
makes Homer almost commonplace; it is hard to realize that
he was a contemporary of the democratic Aeschylus. But in
his conviction of Zeus's concern for human conduct he
stands with Hesiod, and his notions of rewards and punishments in a future existence are more firmly outlined. Here
is Pindar's eschatology, as presented in his Second Olympian
Ode:

But verily, wealth adorned with virtues bringeth the fitting
chance of divers boons, prompting the heart of man to a keen
and eager quest, wealth which is that star conspicuous, that
truest light of man. But if, in very deed, when he hath that
wealth, he knoweth of the future, that immediately after

death, on earth, it is the lawless spirits that suffer punishment—and the sins committed in this realm of Zeus are
judged by One who passeth sentence stern and inevitable;
while the good, having the sun shining for evermore, for equal
nights and equal days, receive the boon of a life of lightened
toil, not vexing the soil with the strength of their hands, no,
nor the water of the sea, to gain a scanty livelihood; but, in
the presence of the honoured gods, all who are wont to re-
joice in keeping their oaths, share a life that knoweth no tears,
while the others endure labour that none can look upon—But,
whosoever, while dwelling in either world, have thrice been
courageous in keeping their souls pure from all deeds of wrong,
pass by the highway of Zeus unto the tower of Cronos, where
the ocean-breezes blow around the Islands of the Blest, and
flowers of gold are blazing, some on the shore from radiant
trees, while others the water fostereth; and with chaplets
thereof they entwine their hands, and with crowns, according
to the righteous councils of Rhadamanthys, who shareth for
evermore the judgment-seat of the mighty Father.

It is a little startling to find wealth so important a criterion,
but it is wealth gotten by individual prowess and spent for
magnificent athletic victories. Toil and expenditure (*ponos*
and *dapane*) are always in Pindar the hallmark of notable
achievement; his is not a world of potters and beggars, but
it sets a high value on free enterprise nevertheless.

The significant thing in the Pindaric passage (and in
similar utterances in Pindar and in other authors) is that it
is not the free fancy of a poet but part of an organized and
to some degree esoteric system. His arrows, Pindar says, are
vocal to the wise, "but for the crowd they need interpreters."
We can see the beginnings of an authoritarian priesthood,
exploiting an esoteric doctrine which it alone controls and

supporting and being supported by an aristocracy which becomes its secular arm. Just such a sequence brought intellectual and social mummification to the Indians, who were of kindred language and presumably stock with the Greeks. If what happened to the Indians would have happened to the Greeks our own civilization would probably have taken on a different complexion, and it is interesting to speculate on the means by which Greek rationalism was preserved. Part of the explanation may be the importance of Homer himself in the education of the Greeks. A more tangible explanation is the westward expansion of Persia, which affected Athenian life in two ways. For one thing, the Greek resistance to Persia depended on class attitudes: oligarchies preferred the domination of Persia, which would preserve their prerogatives, to the rise of democracy. Delphi itself Medized (as it later laconized in the Peloponnesian War) and so did Pindar's Thebes. Democratic Athens resisted, and Aeschylus probably served in the Athenian navy. History affords other examples of throne and altar supporting one another and falling together.

The other direction in which the expansion of Persia may have contributed to the preservation of Greek rationalism was its conquest of the enlightened Greek cities of Asia Minor and the consequent displacement of the Ionian philosophers. Again history affords parallels for refugees from totalitarian conquest affecting the intellectual climate of their new homes. What is common to the Ionian philosophers is their quest for intelligible explanations of phenomena. When the Milesians labored to identify the substratum of the physical world their object may not have been to reduce the realm of the mysterious because it is prolific of irrational belief, but such was their effect nevertheless. When Leucippus and Democritus maintained that the world was made up of atoms and the void they thereby reduced the scope of the divine; the Epicureans who later adopted and popularized the atomic theory did so specifically to eliminate belief in divine interference in the management of the world. Xenophanes not only specifically condemned current theologies but advocated a more exalted one, which gave man greater dignity. He denied that the gods could act dishonorably or have human shape or understanding; instead there is a supreme deity who sways the universe through thought alone. It is significant that the same Xenophanes rejected the view of excellence (*arete*) which is characteristic of Pindar; intellectual achievement, he insisted, is a far more useful thing than athletic prowess.

A certain amount of interaction between what we should call the religious and rationalist tendencies appears in writers of either camp. If, for example, Hesiod presents the religious view, his efforts to impose system and intelligibility, in his *Theogony,* indicate a scientific approach. Empedocles could combine work on physics and work on purifications. But in general, as at other periods, each tendency appears to have followed its own path. Where we should expect collision is in a field like healing the sick, where one group would lean toward religious purifications and the other to rationalist means; and it is in fact in the medical writings of the Hippocratic Corpus, some of which are as early as the fifth century, that we sense explicit conflict between the two. The opening paragraphs of *The Sacred Disease* maintain that this name was given to epilepsy by essentially ignorant men who claimed great piety and superior knowledge. On the basis of this claim they prescribe purifications and cleansings, which are of no value. Mere ignorance of a phenomenon is no sufficient reason for calling it sacred.

Exclusion of other than physiological considerations even in such a disease as epilepsy, which looks like a very clear manifestation of nonphysiological phenomena, is tantamount to a denial of extraphysical considerations in evaluating man generally. So in the Hippocratic treatise *On Air Waters Places* (12 ff.) variations in physique and character between different peoples in Europe, Asia, and Africa are attributed solely, with such "demonstrations as the author is capable of," to variations in geography and climate. The implications are enormous. If only externals set one group apart from another and the basic nature of man is as consistent as his physiology, then not only differences between Greek and barbarian but differences between noble and commoner, the privileged and the humble, are also not inherent but only due to environment. The inherent nature of man is not subject to change, but the environment is; if a barbarian is transplanted to Hellas or a slave to a privileged class he can acquire the usages of his new environment. The Greek word *nomos,* which is usually translated "law," does in fact mean "usage" or "convention."

The distinction between *nomos* and *physis* is made specific in another treatise in the Hippocratic Corpus (*De victu* 1.11): "*Nomos* men make for themselves, without knowing the things about which they legislate; but the *physis* of everything is ordained by the gods. What men legislate never abides the same, whether it is right or wrong: what the gods ordain always abides upright, whether it is right or wrong. That is the difference." It may well be that this dichotomy is itself a product of Sophistic formulation, for, as we shall see, the Sophists made much of it as a basis for their relativistic morality. But it was from the Hippocratic men of science that the notion must originally have come, as is plain from the famous papyrus fragment of the Sophist Antiphon (Diels-Kranz 44 A, 2.353), in which the universality of *physis* is demonstrated by the argument that Hellenes and barbarians breathe alike through nostrils and mouth and take their food alike. The distinction between them is only in *nomos*.

The doctrine that everything outside physiology is merely conventional is potentially subversive in the highest degree. The conventions may have been established unfairly, for class interest, and even if they were once serviceable they may no longer be so, and if they are not they not only may but should be revised. All institutions, all class differentiations, all beliefs must be re-examined every day to see whether they are still serviceable. And no external authority or tradition is relevant to this test. "Man is the measure of all things," said Protagoras; of the gods it was not for him to speak, for he could know nothing of them. We can see why all conservatives feared and hated the Sophists. When Euripides questions the Athenian degradation of women and foreigners, as he does in the *Medea* and elsewhere, or of the illegitimately born, as he does in the *Hippolytus,* he is basing himself on the Sophists' distinction between *physis* and *nomos*. It is only *nomos,* not *physis,* that puts disabilities upon the underprivileged. In the Melian dialogue at the end of Thucydides' fifth book, when the Melians protest that the gods will disapprove of Athenian ruthlessness, the Athenians answer: "Of the gods we believe, and of men we know, that by a necessary law of their *nature* they rule wherever they can." What the gods do can only be surmised and is anyhow irrelevant; the criterion for human conduct is human nature. And this is precisely the position of Thrasymachus in the first book of Plato's *Republic*. It is in the nature of man for might to make right; efforts to ameliorate this law of nature on the basis of any external code of conduct are merely sentimental. Anyone who, like Socrates, clings to these outworn external imperatives should have a nurse to wipe his sniveling nose.

It is important to realize that the Sophist position did not entail disbelief in the gods or even opposition to religion, as it might in an exclusive monotheism with an authoritarian priesthood. *Physis,* as the pseudo-Hippocratic passage indicates, remained in the realm of the gods, and their care of it was from their own point of view (which was all that mattered) correct. Protagoras did declare that "man is the measure of all things," but the most that can be said of his theological position is that he is agnostic: "With regard to the gods I cannot feel sure either that they are or that they are not, nor what they are like in figure; for there are many things that hinder sure knowledge, the obscurity of the subject and the shortness of human life." Even Xenophanes questions only men's conceptions of the gods when he says that cattle and lions would depict gods in their own image if they had hands; not only is he not atheist but he asserts the existence of deity very firmly. So Euripides may criticize men's conceptions, we might even say uses, of the gods, but not their existence or their effectiveness, as plays like the *Bacchae* or the *Hippolytus* make abundantly clear. Neither did Thrasymachus nor the Athenians before Melos deny the existence or efficacy of the gods. They exist and act as becomes gods, not necessarily as men would have them act; what men must do is to act manfully according to men's nature.

Actually, then, the Sophist view is a natural outgrowth of the Homeric. Achilles could well have subscribed to Protagoras' dictum, and the Sophists, by corollary, were only emulating Achilles in a less heroic environment. Achilles had been educated to be a speaker of words and a doer of deeds; in the world of the Sophists if a man perfected himself in the first, which they made it their business to teach, he would be in position to achieve the second. When it is said of them that they made the worse appear the better cause, we need only substitute "weaker" and "stronger" for "worse" and "better." When men had to plead their own cases at law it might promote justice, not subvert it, if an honest but weak speaker could be taught to make his presentation stronger.

And the opponents of the Sophists were the successors of the same anti-Homeric strain which insisted that Zeus had 30,000 agents to keep watch over men so that he could dispense rewards and punishments. For the dualism of body and soul which this view posits, with its concomitant that the body is to be suppressed in the interest of the ascent of the soul, the greatest and most eloquent spokesman is of course Plato—who might himself be regarded as a Sophist except for the central conviction. In view of Plato's towering stature, and, more important, in view of the indubitably Greek antecedents of his thought, it is absurd to dismiss him, as has sometimes been done, as "an alien drop in the Greek blood-stream." But if we consider Homer as repre-

senting the authentic peculiarly Greek view, Plato is in fact
a deviation. Unquestioning submission to a spiritual authority and aspiration toward an undefined goal is not what sets
the Greeks apart from other men.

When Greek ways spread to the east in the Hellenistic
age Plato himself was probably the greatest single agent of
Hellenization. His doctrine, on politics as well as on the
soul, was so sympathetic to the peoples of the east that in
their desire to claim cultural precedence over the Greeks
one after another of these peoples claimed that he had
learned it from their own sages. But in Greece itself, apparently, Plato's influence was limited. His Academy was,
as we shall see, exclusive and to a degree esoteric. Virtually
all of the literary figures of the next generation were alumni
not of the Academy but of the school of Isocrates, out of
which they emerged, as Cicero remarked, like the army of
heroes out of the Trojan horse. Aristotle's Lyceum appears
to have been even more specialist and equally exclusive. It
was the Aristotelian organization of learning, to be sure, that
was taken up by the Alexandrian savants, but Aristotle himself is virtually unheard of in the Hellenistic age and was
revived only in the Roman period.

The most widespread philosophic tendencies of the Hellenistic age were the Stoic and the Epicurean. Stoicism
differs from Platonism in many respects, but it is like Platonism and indeed surpasses it in advocating cultivation of
the soul and suppression of the body, envisaging an exclusive perfectionism, prescribing an ascent of the soul to union
with the divine. It may be significant that the leading
teachers of Stoicism came from areas under eastern influence.

Epicureanism, which preceded Stoicism in time, was an Athenian phenomenon, and it arose and was developed in calculated opposition to Platonism. What it amounted to, in essence, was a return to the materialistic physical theories of atomism advanced by the pre-Socratics Democritus and Leucippus, and to the principle of the disparate spheres of gods and men reflected in Homer. Indeed, the latter is their more important theory, and the physics mainly a device to provide a rational scaffolding for it. The Epicureans have had a blacker reputation than the Sophists because both Christianity and Rome, who provide the bulk of the literary record, considered them dangerously subversive. Any system based upon a divine sanction must have so considered them, and they were indeed a danger, for they enjoyed an enormous following over a long period. But just as it is false to accuse them of a sensual program of eating, drinking, and being merry, so it is false to accuse them of atheism, or even of agnosticism. They did specifically believe in the existence of the gods and even urged that the customary rituals be observed; what they denied was that the gods had any special concern for the affairs of men, that they were accessible to prayer, or that they kept watch over men's behavior and would dispense rewards and punishments. It was to allay fear of such punishment that the Epicureans insisted that the soul was material and that its atoms dispersed along with those of the body. The soul is not a separate entity but part of man's physiology. The gods were off beyond man's ken, having a divine time; it would be a contradiction to conceive of them as laboring in man's interests. When Lucretius, Epicurus' fullest spokesman, inveighs against religion, it is men's wrong conceptions of the gods, not the gods themselves, that he is speaking of. *Tantum religio potuit suadere malorum* means not "the gods caused evil so great" but "to evil so great did religious institutions *persuade* men."

Just as Epicurus' atomic theory derived directly from the pre-Socratics so did his view of the gods derive from Homer. For him Plato was indeed a deviation from the central stream of Greek thought. If the Homeric view of the gods is in fact as it has been outlined in a previous chapter, then Epicurus' doctrine may be considered a philosophic formulation of what Homer believed. As we can see both from Homer's heroes and from such true Epicureans as we know, it was a belief which released men, endowed them with individual responsibility and the incentive to realize such excellence as they were capable of, and did not deprive the world of gods whom men might even love if they did not expect to be loved in return.

VII.

The Cult of Hellenism

BECAUSE the Greeks were polytheists, and because there was no single organized cult (as there might have been if the Orphics had a missionary urge and had succeeded in it) capable of suppressing dissidents, the Olympian and Chthonic trends, if we may still call them so, continued to survive side by side. And both were perpetuated in the European tradition. For the survival of the Chthonic-Orphic complex we have not far to seek. It may be, as many scholars maintain, that the Aegean civilization out of which they sprang was shared by peoples east of the Mediterranean, so that the same complex of beliefs developed independently in the Near East. In historical times, in any case, and specifically in the Hellenistic period, there was much ideological interaction between east and west, and the influence of Platonism and of Stoicism is palpable in Hellenistic Judaism and in Christianity. For the survival of this complex, therefore, we need look no further than the Judaeo-Christian tradition.

But what of the Olympians? Did the outlooks associated with them also persist, and if so, how did they survive the competition of the Platonic tradition? In part, certainly, through the tendency for an established ethos to persist, and through the influence of a highly regarded literature which embodied the Olympian outlook. Homer continued to be the one book everyone knew, and if no new great tragedies were written the old continued to be acted and studied. But the means which men ordinarily use for transmitting a particular set of values is formal education. It happens that we are in position to examine educational theory at a period when rival teachers were conscious of their opposition and presumably eager to propagate each his own view.

The first educational institutions in Europe recognizably like our own were two established in Athens early in the fourth century B.C., by Plato and by Isocrates. What went on inside Plato's Academy we can only surmise, but the theory and objectives of his educational system are quite clear. We know, for example, that specialization was a cardinal principle in his social thinking. Cobblers must stick to their last and not meddle with flute-playing, or flautists with training horses, and so forth. But neither could a man participate in government or read books except under specialist direction. For his ideal polity, indeed, Plato would ordain a strict censorship of books. Homer would be banned because he inculcates wrong views of the gods and because Achilles, whom readers might be moved to emulate, is too headstrong. For training the intellect the Academy relied on a vigorous course of mathematics, not what we should call the humanities. And Plato's system was exclusive in another respect. In his autobiographical Seventh Epistle he declares that any man who claims that he has learned his doctrine from books is lying, for it could be learned only by long personal association with the master, from whom it was communicated as by a spark. Only an elect was eligible for such an education.

Aristotle was one of the elect who maintained personal association with Plato for twenty years, and then found himself at odds with the master. But in respect to educational theory Aristotle went beyond Plato in specialization. Aristotle's school was in effect a series of research institutes of advanced grade, each investigating some special field of knowledge by something resembling the method of the biologist. The work they did was of a high order of professional competence, but there is no evidence that it reached very far beyond the walls of the school. The heirs of Aristotle's research institutes were the Library and Museum in Alexandria, which were even more insulated from the world. Even literary men, who were now pensioners of the Ptolemies, had no real audience but addressed each other. As Timon said of them, they were birds fattened in a coop. Professionalization, with the consequent abdication of ordinary men, becomes apparent in all cultural pursuits: in Athens of the classical period a man was expected to be able to accompany himself on a musical instrument—now he must be a virtuoso; he was expected to perform competently on the athletic field— now he must be a champion; he was expected to read books—now he must be a philologer.

The school of Isocrates had different objectives and different techniques. For considerable stretches his thought is parallel to Plato's—one is tempted to say, where Plato is representing the true Socrates; the differences appear to come when Plato leaves Socrates behind. In Plato's *Phaedrus* Isocrates is called a "companion" of Socrates, who is quoted as prosphesying a distinguished future for him. And he shows the influence of Socrates not only in such traits as aloofness from public life, critical attitude toward the democracy, and hatred of demagogues but also in his view on education. He despises the pretensions of the Sophists (though he himself taught "culture" for pay), he regards speculation on the origin of things as useless, he is deeply concerned for ethics and high morality. Exact sciences he thinks useful only as a preparatory mental discipline; and speculative philosophy he regards as worse than useless. Dialectic which pretends to attain truth in disregard of the facts of human nature (he calls such dialectic "eristic," or competitive) he condemns, as he does Sophists who aim for sensational effects. They pretend to be able to teach what in fact cannot be taught, and the practical oratory they teach deals not with large ideas but with petty controversies; and because its goal is success rather than truth, it is immoral.

Isocrates' own theory of education is the cultivation of *logos*. The basic meaning of *logos* is "word," but it also means composition, story, rationale, and in particular the art of discourse. *Logos* is almost a living entity, not nearly so definite or so mystical as the *logos* of Christianity, but ready to move in that direction. It implies reason, feeling, imagination—all that raises men above animal nature and enables them to live a civilized life. Greek is to barbarian as man is to animal. As men's pre-eminence over animals consists in his possession of *logos,* so the Greek is superior because he knows many *logoi*. The more words and discourses a man knows, the richer his experience and ability to think, and therefore the more human he is. Specialized and theoretical knowledge are disparaged because they do not contribute, as humanistic education does, to the practical conduct of human relations.

When Isocrates says "Greek" he does not limit its application to racial Hellenes. Greek is defined, he says (*Pan-*

egyricus 50), not by race but by education. Humanistic
education is not then an exclusive possession of Hellenes
but accessible to all men who wish to participate in what
the Greeks regard as education. Education is not training
for a craft or profession or any specialty but familiarity with
a traditional library of books—the same library, in effect,
which continued to be the mainstay of liberal education in
the Hellenistic world, in Rome, and, with vicissitudes of
fortune, in Europe to this day.

What such an education could be expected to yield we
can gather from Isocrates' own quite abundant literary remains and from various fourth-century authors who had
been his pupils. In the first place he insisted that prose discourse must be artistic and introduced a series of stylistic
refinements which made of prose an art form almost as
precise and demanding as poetry. He rigidly avoids hiatus
and harsh clashes of consonants; the rhythms of clauses are
carefully balanced; sentences are constructed with nice attention to their architecture, and single periods run to long
paragraphs. In the Greek view, it must be remembered, the
poet was an artistic creator, not necessarily in verse, and he
regarded himself, and was regarded by his audience, as a
serious teacher. "Boys in school have a master to teach
them," Aeschylus is made to say in Aristophanes' *Frogs,*
"we poets are the teachers of men." Isocrates maintained
that since prose had now become artistic there was no more
need for verse, and in fact Greeks apparently ceased writing
serious verse until it was revived, as a tour de force, in the
Hellenistic age. What we have, between the fifth century
and Alexandria, are verse drama, which was required for

the religious festivals, such useful genres as epigrams for epitaphs and ex-votos, and songs.

Isocrates' views of history and politics are more significant. He himself wrote no history but only Orations, or more properly essays, but these and the work of the historians who were his pupils show where he stood. In the first place Isocrates made of history an art, not a science as Aristotle would have had it. This implied not only a high concern for rhetorical style but also heightening the reader's interest by all the devices appropriate to melodrama and arousing his pity and fear. But Isocrates also wished to make history edifying, and to this end he took a new attitude toward tradition. In his own writings we can see a new tendency to idealize the past and make of it an armory of examples for guiding political attitudes and actions in the present. The past came to be considered a guide to the future more literally than it had ever been before. And finally, it was Isocrates who promoted the practice of glorifying individual figures as catalysts of history. This is not merely another aspect of his idealization of the past but a concept of how history is made. Furthermore, it is an assertion of the principle of recognizing and encouraging high achievement.

The central conviction which informed Isocrates' political teaching, and certainly the most significant for posterity, is the view of Hellenism which exalts it to the position of a religion and which gives the character of a crusade to efforts to preserve and propagate it. Hellenism was indeed endangered by the series of ruinous wars which followed the Peloponnesian, and the only way to counter fragmentation was a purposeful drive toward consolidation. Isocrates based his pleas for union on the ground of survival; only the realization of community of cultural interests which transcended local political differences could protect Hellenism from external dangers. In the *Panegyricus,* written in 380 B.C., Isocrates calls for concord among the confederated Greeks, under the leadership of Athens, for the purpose of making war against Persia, which was a standing threat to Hellenism. When the passing years held out little hope that voluntary union could be achieved, Isocrates addressed an appeal, in 356, to Archidamus III, King of Sparta, to lead a Panhellenic war against Persia. In 346, in his Address to Philip, he appeals to the Macedonian to lead the great crusade. But other Greek patriots, and specifically Demosthenes, saw a graver peril to Greek freedom in Philip than in the Persian, and in any case a ruthless conqueror who ruled a people excluded from the Delphian games because they were not authentic Hellenes seems an odd sort of champion for Hellenism.

The issue between Demosthenes and Isocrates is a permanent one in politics; at several conjunctures of history it has become acute, and not least in our own day. Honest men have espoused one side or the other, and Isocrates has been praised or condemned according to prevailing political climates. Admirers of fifth-century Athens can only sympathize with Demosthenes' efforts to preserve its traditional values pure by absolute independence, and yet it was Isocrates who more clearly discerned the wave of the future and strove to encompass it for the survival of cultural values; partisans of Isocrates who condemn Demosthenes as an unseasonable romantic have a plausible case. In any event, Philip became master by knocking his opponents' heads together at Chaeronea in 336, and when his son Alexander proceeded to his conquests of Persia he advertised his campaigns as Greek victories and was careful to send official reports of them to Athens. It should be noted, however, that when Alexander's agent Antipater finally dictated terms to Athens in 322 B.C. not only were its democratic institutions abolished, but of its 21,000 citizens 12,000 who did not possess property to the value of 2,000 drachmas were disenfranchised and deported as being a turbulent element, and the 9,000 richest citizens who constituted the "party of order" were left in possession.

Alexander's achievement, both in respect to military victory and, far more significantly, in respect to the new impulse and new directions for the survival of Hellenism, constitute the most spectacular demonstration of the soundness of Isocrates' program. Alexander's own teacher Aristotle was to all appearances totally unaware that the world was being revolutionized. His political studies are premised on the unexamined assumption that the old order of disparate city states was permanent. Alexander, at least after his initial victories, envisioned and sought to promote a harmonious unison of the whole of the civilized world.

Of all the material achievements of Greece its cultural penetration of the Near East in the century after Alexander is the most impressive. For scale the only analogous example of cultural imperialism is the spread of European culture in America; but whereas English settlers found only scattered aborigines in the Neolistic stage of development the Greeks came into a country crowded with the descendants of highly civilized peoples from whose ancestors they had themselves learned. To be sure, the process had started much earlier;

Greek merchants carried their enterprise far and wide and Greek mercenaries and artisans appear in unlikely places. In the fifth century B.C. coins struck at Jerusalem imitate Greek types. But after Alexander what had been a trickle became a flood. So far from resisting the new ways the natives, especially of the upper classes, were eager to embrace them. Greek was the language of government, of business, and of fashion, and ancient cities were turned into Greek poleis (sometimes paying for the privilege) and adopted the institutions and ways of life of the Greek city. Natives wrote books in Greek, and even when, for religious reasons, they wrote in native tongues, they adopted Greek literary modes. A work like the First Book of the Maccabees, which was written in Hebrew to glorify a war against a "Greek" king, shows how deeply Hellenism had penetrated. Not only does the form plainly show the influence of Hellenistic historiography, but the war itself starts with rivalry for the high priesthood waged by two men each of whom bore a Greek name and both of whom were eager to adopt Greek ways of life. The struggle was not *against* Hellenism but to attain a sovereignty like others that were arising from the debris of the Seleucid empire. Until the end of the first century A.D. the Jews were as receptive to Hellenism as any other eastern people.

The quality of the Greek precipitate in the provinces of the Greek cultural empire and the channels by which Greek outlooks were incorporated into the main stream of European culture we shall glance at presently. What was transmitted, naturally, was neither of the classical Greek strains separately—Chthonic or Olympian, mystic or rational, Platonic or Isocratean—but an amalgam compounded of the two along with new ingredients contributed by the subjects of the cultural empire. But the strand we have called Olympian remains recognizable even in the amalgam, and indeed until the compound was fixed by Christianity the outlines of the conflict between the intellectual successors of the Chthonic and Olympian parties are sharper than they appeared to be in the classical period.

The articulate spokesmen of the later fourth century—historians, orators, statesmen—were alumni not of Plato's school but of Isocrates'. These men participated in and gave direction to political and intellectual life; the disciples of Plato were specifically philosophers, and increasingly what we should call closet philosophers. The school of Aristotle fell into almost complete oblivion and scarcely affected the thought of the Hellenistic age. This was dominated by the Stoics and the Epicureans, who were alike in their general object of making men spiritually at home in a world grown overwhelmingly large and oppressive, but whose philosophical outlooks were essentially different—far more different than the outlooks of Platonist and Aristotelian.

The Epicureans came first in time, probably had a wider following, and persisted as a distinct school, with their philosophy unaltered, for a longer period. The initial motivation of Epicureanism was apparently opposition to Platonism; at least each of their tenets is a direct denial of some Platonic position. The core of the matter is the refutation of dualism. The Epicureans speak of a soul, of course, for in Greek usage soul signifies *all* that distinguishes a live man from a corpse. But for the Epicureans the soul, like the body, is composed of atoms, and these are dispersed at death. Just as the soul has no kind of existence separate from the body's, so it has no separate loyalty, no obligation to follow a code different from the body's. In an absolute sense man is the measure, and the sole measure. The only criterion for conduct is pleasure, which is defined as the absence of pain; naturally a sensible man will avoid indulgences which entail pain that outweighs the pleasure they give, and in fact the Epicureans whom we know were far from being libertines. Divine retribution was out of the question—in a future existence because there is none, and in the present existence because the gods (who do indeed exist) are indifferent to the doings of man. There was no blessed age in the past from which man degenerated, and there will be none in the future to which man may aspire. Political institutions and the structure of society are not divinely ordained and possess no sacred authority. They are the creations of men, devised to make life safer and more agreeable, and they are to be preserved only because they perform these functions.

As has been suggested in an earlier chapter, there is nothing here that is not a legitimate outgrowth from the premises of Homer, refined and systematized, to be sure, in more sophisticated centuries, and with outlines sharpened by rivalry with an equally systematized opposition. Epicureanism was anathema to Platonists and eventually to Christians, for whom reality resided in an unseen world; it was officially anathema to the Jews, who made *epikoros* the word for the, to them, novel concept of infidel; and it became anathema to the rulers of Rome, whose authority was made to rest upon a religious sanction. But unlike other systems, which trimmed or extended their original principles to meet emergent needs or survive competition, Epicureanism remained consistently itself to the end. In an essay of Plutarch's, representatives of various schools defer to one another in discussion in an effort to reach some acceptable compromise; the Epicurean says his piece and departs, for there is no way the starkness of his system can be mitigated without being fatally compromised.

It was not only the otherworldliness of Plato's system that the Epicureans opposed; they reacted as strongly against its exclusiveness. Lucretius is doubtless an extreme example of the evangelical zeal of the Epicureans, but an evangelical impulse is apparent in the school from the beginning. If distinctions of place and rank have no valid external sanction and each individual is an autarchic entity, then each is entitled to the advantages of education and must be invited to participate in them according to his will and capacity. Where Plato insisted that his doctrine could be learned only by personal contact, not from books, Epicurus pioneered in democratizing knowledge through textbooks, even graded textbooks, the Lesser Epitome and the Greater. And we know that the Epicurean doctrine did indeed spread very widely; it was the official philosophy of the Seleucid court and it had numerous and distinguished adherents in Rome until it was officially frowned upon.

In its efforts to make itself accessible to all men Stoicism was like Epicureanism, and indeed its philosophy provided a more exigent rationale for evangelism. If men are all members of one another and all equally portions of the divine then the career of Stoic Sage, which is to be attained by laboriously purging away the perturbations which hamper the rise of the soul, is open to all, without distinction of place or rank. We may hazard the conjecture that this particular, and important, aspect of Stoicism was a contribution of the non-Platonic strand in Greek thought. It was the Hippocratics, as we have noted above, who used physiology to prove that differences among men were due to environment, and Antiphon, who used the arguments to show that Hellenes and barbarians were not essentially different. Isocrates could then define Hellene not by race but by education. The direct antecedents of the Stoics were the Cynics, and it was Diogenes of Sinope, the original Cynic, who declared that he was a *cosmopolites* or citizen of the world. Diogenes' remark amounted to a beggar's truculent refusal to recognize the superiority of privileged citizenship, but his nobly born and gentle disciple Crates gave the notion of universal citizenship a positive rather than negative value, and Crates was the teacher of Zeno.

Stoicism is thus itself an example of the fusion of the two Greek strands, and an important example because of its influence upon Christianity and upon Rome. Indeed the passion for righteousness which characterizes the early Stoa (but grew paler as Stoics learned to abate their perfectionism and come to terms with the world) may itself have derived from the early teachers of Stoicism, who were men from the eastern Mediterranean. But though Stoicism assigned the individual a higher dignity than Platonism had done and virtually equated the world with Zeus and providence, yet in making the body a hindrance to the soul and in promising souls purified union with the divine it follows the Orphic rather than the Olympian strain. Through its otherworldly appeal when men were eager for external support and through its influence upon Christianity and upon Rome it far overshadowed Epicureanism, and in itself, so far as men of the eighteenth century could enucleate it from certain Lives of Plutarch, it contributed an impulse to the French Revolution; but it is Epicureanism rather than Stoicism that is the true representative of the authentic Hellenic tradition.

The universalist principles of Stoicism and Epicureanism alike transcended the limitations of Greek geography and race, but though their doctrines and Greek ways generally had penetrated far to the east and the west, Greece itself, its character and its history, became a shining ideal to which all civilized men paid reverence. But how could the ideal survive political realities? After Alexander Greece had been subject to Alexander's successors, and from the second century B.C. onward it was subject, beyond the remotest hope of liberation, to the enormously more powerful dominion of Rome. It is understandable that a highly civilized subject people might affect a less advanced conqueror, but it is hard to conceive that the subjugated people should survive as an ideal. What enabled the Greek ideal to survive was its detachment from national sovereignty and its transformation into something like a religious cult, and one capable of making converts *in partibus infidelium*.

The achievement is remarkable enough, but not so remarkable as it would seem in the light of the intense nationalism of modern times with its concomitant axiom that a suzerain people is culturally superior to its satellites and justifies colonialism as a civilizing mission. Greek city-states too were fiercely exclusive, but from the beginning Hellene pride rested on being Hellene rather than on being a citizen of a powerful state. In Homer what chiefly sets the Greeks apart as a group is their common enterprise against Troy.

They are not markedly different from the Trojans in character, and amongst themselves there is no sense of common loyalty strong enough to prevent an Achilles from withdrawing from the enterprise or to condemn him for his withdrawal. Language, religion, and shared ideals did indeed create a sense of kinship among all Greeks, and in wars with each other they did observe certain decencies which they did not observe in war against barbarians and condemned violation of these decencies as un-Greek. But they could unite for common action, and only precariously, only against a common danger, as in the Persian wars; and even so each party to an intra-Hellenic conflict was ready to invite non-Hellenic assistance against a Hellenic enemy. Any common action that was undertaken was undertaken by an alliance of sovereign peers rather than by a single sovereign state. Within the Hellene name differences so antipodal as those between democratic Athens and authoritarian Sparta would have made genuine political union impossible. Always, then, it was a cultural ideal rather than a political organism that gave the classical Greeks their essential unity. The same Isocrates who called for a Greek crusade against Persia defined Greek not by political allegiance or even race but by culture.

Just as the Persian invasions had created an ephemeral Greek unity in the early fifth century B.C., so did Roman domination in the second. At first one Greek confederacy was very ready to invite Roman assistance against a rival Greek confederacy. But the chafed Romans soon gave up the fiction of being liberators and became open masters. In 146 B.C. they destroyed Corinth, and they made their mastery more unmistakable yet when Mithridates of Pontus, posing as the champion of Hellenism, induced Athens to revolt in 88 B.C. Unity was thus imposed from above—on political ciphers. Now all Greeks who valued Hellenism could unite in high pride in the Greek experience and achievement in the past, and this they could do with assurance because the more intelligent of their conquerors admired the Greek achievement also and sought out Greek artists and philosophers and poets.

To say that Hellenism, after all hope of political independence had vanished, was transformed into a cult is something more than hyperbole. The position became very like that of Christianity in countries where Church and State are separate. What the cult demanded may be seen from the career of such an ardent and articulate adherent as Plutarch. Of Plutarch we know that he gave up a successful career in Rome itself to return to provincial Chaeronea, that he accepted a minor local magistracy there and a priesthood in the obsolescent shrine of Delphi, that he gathered the young men of his neighborhood to discourse to them of literature and philosophy and music. The only reason for a man of Plutarch's position to do these things is that to do them is to do what a man who revered the Greek way must do. A Greek must participate in government, and if he could not be archon at Athens he must follow the form by being market inspector at Chaeronea. If there was one single symbol of Hellenism it was Delphi, and a Greek must do what he could to revitalize that symbol. And most of all, he must initiate the young into the cultural legacy of Hellenism. Readers have wondered why the *Parallel Lives* include only statesmen and generals, not philosophers and artists. The reason is simple. Greek cultural superiority did not have to be emphasized for all the world acknowledged it; but even Greeks, after two centuries of Roman domination, accepted the superiority of the Romans in war and government, and so it was a service to Hellenism to remind its adherents that Pericles and Alexander were at least comparable to Fabius and Caesar.

And the cult was capable of missionary activity. No contemporary could imagine that the Roman Empire would ever end, and Plutarch was very ready to accept Rome's services in policing and administering the world; but Rome itself might be more fully evangelized to propagate Hellenism. It is significant that Plutarch exerts himself to assimilate cults of peoples susceptible to Hellenism, like the Egyptian Isis and Osiris, to the cult of Apollo; he condemns the religious observances of the Jews and the Carthaginians as superstitions because these could not be assimilated to the Greek way. If today we still admire and study the Greeks it is partly because men like Plutarch did raise Hellenism to a cult independent of national sovereignty.

When the multifarious experiences of an idealized past are transformed into something like a cult discrepancies are smoothed over and the whole reduced to a consistent mass. So the manifold experiences of the Hebrews were molded into the cult of Judaism; the conduct of some of the patriarchs may not have jibed with the ethical teachings of the prophets or the practices of the priests, but they are mortised into the cult Hagiographa nevertheless. Now Plutarch's own philosophy was consistently Platonist, and his attitude to Plato, who deviated from the principal made central in these pages, was nothing short of reverent. His essay *On Love,* for example, concludes by celebrating conjugal love, in keeping with his own temper and the temper of his age, but for all his discomfort in so doing he scrupulously reproduces the viewpoint of Plato's *Symposium* also. As we should expect, he frowns on Stoicism and is expressly antagonistic to Epicureanism. And yet Stoicism and even Epicureanism have their place within the body of Hellenism; we might almost apply the rabbinic formula for reconciling differences of opinion: "These words and those alike are words of the living God."

But Plutarch's deviation from Plato in another respect, and the plainest manifestation of the principle of Hellenism we are here concerned with, is to be seen in his interest in biography. Herodotus declared that he wrote his history to preserve the memory of men's great deeds from oblivion, and the motive in the biographies of Plutarch (who disliked Herodotus for maligning his native Boeotia) appears to be the same. To preserve the record of high individual achievement in the past is important in itself and it is important too as an example and incentive to emulation. As has been suggested in an earlier chapter, the significant change brought in by the Middle Ages, from the viewpoint of this essay, was a new anonymity to replace individual pride of achievement. The great vogue which Plutarch's *Lives* (not his more extensive *Moralia*) enjoyed in the humanist age was surely due in no small part to the fact that they did provide records of high achievement and examples for emulation. Except for lives of saints, which belong to a different category, there is no such series of *Lives* between Plutarch's and Vasari's. The men of the Renaissance took up just where the Greeks had left off.

VIII.

Channels to Europe

FROM late antiquity to modern times there has been no absolute break in the stream of European culture. The whole Mediterranean and its appanages were more or less thoroughly Hellenized, and outsiders who impinged upon the main stream, whether the Arian vandals who sacked Rome, or the Mohammedans, or the Slavs, had themselves been tinctured with Hellenism. But though in its totality the movement forward, with wide differences in pace and thoroughness, is a continuum, for purposes of simplification three main channels may be discerned: the Judaeo-Christian tradition, Rome, and the Greek tradition unqualified as it was understood in the Renaissance and in the eighteenth century.

To begin with the first, Greek influence upon Judaism has been shown by modern scholarship to have been much more pervasive than had previously been suspected; more of the Hellenistic element in Christianity was taken over from Judaism, which had already assimilated it, than adopted directly from the Greeks. Archaeology has demonstrated a potent and continuous Greek influence in the environs of Jerusalem itself from the fifth century B.C. onward, and the later books of the Old Testament canon, to say nothing of the Apocrypha and other intertestamentary writings, exhibit clear signs of Greek influence. It is altogether probable that Chronicles is influenced by Hellenistic historiography, Job by tragedy, Canticles by Hellenistic erotic poetry, Jonah by aretology, Ecclesiastes by Epicureanism and the diatribe form. Of this group the books which, form aside, communicate the Greek outlooks which here concern us are in the first instance Job, and then Ecclesiastes.

Job presents a thoroughly tragic view of life, with the human and divine spheres disparate and with man left to achieve his own destiny in despite of the inscrutable interference of the divine. Man is born to sorrow as the sparks fly upward. And if Job reflects the essentially Greek view at the tragic level Ecclesiastes does so at the Epicurean. It is indeed more assertively Epicurean than Job is tragic. The fool and the wise man, the righteous and the sinner die alike, and the moral is that "there is nothing better for a man than that he should eat and drink and that he should make his soul enjoy good in his labor" (2.24). "For the living know that they shall die, but the dead know not anything, neither have they any more a reward; for the memory of them is forgotten. Also their love and their hatred and their envy is now perished; neither have they any more a portion for ever in anything that is done under the sun" (9.5–6). The moral is not only to eat and drink and be merry but "Whatsoever thy hand findeth to do do it with thy might; for there is no work nor device nor knowledge, nor wisdom in the grave whither thou goest" (9.10). This is as unlike the exhortations of the prophets as it is like the characteristic Greek outlook. Because the Greeks set about doing with all their might what their hands found to do, accepting divine intervention as an ineluctable hazard, not as a law and promise, they were able to achieve the things they did achieve.

When we reflect that the criterion for including books in the canon was the religious principle, the presence of so secular an outlook in a canonical book is remarkable—even if we are religiously admonished in the last two verses of Ecclesiastes: "Let us hear the conclusion of the whole matter: Fear God and keep his commandments, for this is the whole duty of man. For God shall bring every work into judgment, with every secret thing, whether it be good, or whether it be evil." In the intertestamentary period the religious principle is more exigent, for the preservation of books if not for literary productivity as a whole, and the presence of a pronounced secular outlook in some of them is at least as remarkable. What we find, in the extracanonical books, is a tension between the worldly and the otherworldly quite analogous to the tension in classical Greece. It may of course be that the tension is a natural development, independent of the Greek experience; but in view of the penetration of Greek thought and ways of life it is surely easier to regard it as a local variation.

For the specifically religious element (which was largely incorporated into Christianity) we have a "mystical" factor, expressed in numerous apocalypses with their eschatological speculations, and a "rational" factor, expressed in such work as Wisdom of Solomon, IV Maccabees, and the writings of Philo. The latter were palpably influenced by Plato, but it is not unlikely that eschatology was also. Aside from such literary patterns as the Vision of Er at the end of the *Republic,* there is a new conception of *individual* survival for the righteous; earlier hopes for the future had envisaged only the survival of the righteous community.

From the viewpoint of this essay this innovation is of the highest importance. We have seen that the conception of corporate responsibility characteristic of the Chthonian view was refined, for example in the *Oresteia,* to the conception of individual responsibility. It is in keeping with the emphasis on the individual that Pythagoreanism, the mysteries, and Plato envisaged the future destiny of each individual severally, not as part of a group. In the Renaissance, we shall observe, the conception of individual immortality was part of the new emphasis on individual excellence generally, and it is very likely that it was so in the intertestamentary period also. It may be then that the very notion of personal immortality is in itself an expression, within the anti-Olympian view, of the characteristic Greek concern with the individual.

For the worldly element the best document is Ecclesiasticus, which breathes a peculiarly Attic atmosphere. In the first place the author of Ecclesiasticus is unique in his kind in presenting his own personality so fully. We shall see that it is characteristic of the European humanists that they chafed at anonymity and insisted on signing their products. Our author introduces himself (at 50.27) as Jesus son of Sirach of Jerusalem and speaks of himself elsewhere also. He is a learned and experienced man, conscious of his own attainments. His code is enlightened self-interest. He is concerned for the orderly functioning of society and for specialization and high competence among craftsmen. The familiar eulogy of famous men (44.1 ff.) recognizes not only effective administrators, counsellors, and orators, but also "such as found out musical tunes and recited verses in writing." He is aware that the law of the Most High and his covenant must be recognized, and is concerned for religious truth and observance, but his emphasis is on the worldly wisdom that comes from experience. For instance, as we read at 38.1–15, if a man is sick he should pray, cleanse his heart from sin, and offer sacrifice—but he must put himself into the hands of a physician.

This program is quite in keeping with the spirit of classical Greece. What a man must do, recognizing the claims of the divine, is to achieve the excellence which he is capable of and which will bring him personal glory. Indeed, the emphasis on the satisfactions of the individual is the more striking because the demands of the supernatural are now clearly defined, unified, and more exigent. Despite the admonition to prayer and sacrifice, the realms of the human and the divine are delimited; Ajax or Protagoras or Epicurus would also observe the decencies in the matter of prayer and sacrifice, but each depended upon himself to attain his own excellence and to win fame among men.

In other works, and increasingly as time went on, the balance was disrupted as the divine side of the scale came to be more heavily weighted and the human less. From this point of view the course of events in the west was exactly analogous. If the range of achievement of the great figures of the Roman republic was more limited than in Greece, the assertion of individual excellence seems to have been no less important. The Augustan reforms transmuted the Empire to a religious ideal; to serve this ideal is to serve universal destiny, so that patriotism becomes a religious duty. The historians of the Empire are willing enough to recognize high attainments of the heroes of the Republic, but in keep-

ing with the new position of Rome as the divinely chosen
instrument of destiny the motivation for individual achievement is always represented as patriotic. Achilles sulking
when his side needs him is Achilles still; Aeneas is so far the
slave of duty that though he is tempted to indulge his individual desires he may not disregard the course prescribed
for him. He is indeed so far an authentic hero, not a puppet,
in that he is self-impelled to great action and is even concerned for personal glory; but his achievement and his glory
are modes of serving a higher cause.

Retrojectively, in the view which Augustan propaganda
made official, not Aeneas alone but all the great personages
of early Rome, historical as well as legendary, were glorified
only as they served the destiny of Rome. The walls of the
grand Forum which Augustus built were filled with niches
each of which held the bust of a great general who had
triumphed for Rome. The Elysian Fields which Vergil describes in the sixth *Aeneid* do have a small place for pure
priests and noble poets and inventors who had enriched
civilization, but these come as an afterthought to political
personages, and the places of honor are reserved for the
roster of Roman military heroes. Similarly the spacious history of Livy, which is the prose analogue of the *Aeneid,*
glorifies only statesmen or generals who served the state
directly. We think by contrast of the *Parian Chronicle,*
which was short enough to be inscribed on stone and yet
found room to include the victors at Athenian tragic contests. Plutarch had to limit his *Parallel Lives* to statesmen
and warriors, as we have noted, for the record showed no
Roman capable of being matched with Greeks in other
fields. Perhaps the best commentary on the Roman criterion

of excellence is Machiavelli's *Discourses on the First Decade of Livy,* where each of the Roman figures is assessed solely on the basis of his effectiveness in promoting the Roman discipline. It is significant that no Roman writers but only Greeks show appreciation for honest deviationists like the Gracchi.

As the institutions of the Empire hardened and the absolutism of the autocracy became manifest the scope for individual achievement was in fact reduced. Even in the Republic the normal path to distinction was through political activity, but there was room for individualism, as the careers of the Gracchi or of Cicero show. When Cicero was forced out of political life and took to writing philosophical essays he found it necessary to exculpate himself on the ground that such writing too was a service to the state: Romans had been so preoccupied with doing that they had neglected writing, and now that he was excluded from higher service to the state he would devote himself to the lesser service of supplying this want. In the Empire the business of administration was carried out by civil servants and the business of defense by career officers. There was no room for individual opinion on any public issue. A literary career might still win a man a limited kind of fame, but the concern of literature was euphuism or archaism and safe subjects from Greek mythology.

Individualism did assert itself again, in *behalf* of the Roman system, when in the fourth century the inroads of Christianity seemed to threaten traditional Roman values, cultural as well as social and political. The best representative of the adherents of the ancient ideals was Symmachus, the foremost orator and litterateur of his day, and the best

illustration of the quality and course of the conflict is the
fate of the statue of Victory, in fact little more than a symbol of empire, which had always had its place in the Roman
senate house. The statue was removed by Constantine in
357, restored by Julian called the Apostate, and again removed by Gratian in 382. St. Ambrose procured that the
pagan senators who petitioned for its restoration were denied an audience. They petitioned again to Valentinian II
in 384, their spokesman being Symmachus. Symmachus'
usual style is euphuistic in the extreme, filled with jingles
and strained conceits. "The luxuriancy of Symmachus,"
Gibbon wrote, "consists in barren leaves without fruit and
even without flowers. Few facts and few sentiments can be
extracted from his verbose correspondence." But his plea on
behalf of Rome rises to impassioned eloquence. He acknowl-
edges that Victory might be looked upon as a *nomen* rather
than a *numen,* but the *nomen* itself is sacred. Rome herself
is represented as crying out against the death sentence of the
values for which she was guardian and symbol. It required
the energetic intervention of the powerful Ambrose to avert
a pagan victory. The statue was restored during the rebel-
lion of Arbogast and Eugenius in 393 and finally removed
by Theodosius in 394.

Despite Symmachus' protestations that Victory was a
secular symbol, the basis of his plea was in fact religious.
Rome had in fact become a spiritual ideal, and as such
could claim a devotion which it had no power to exact. It is
significant of Symmachus' convictions that he exerted himself to multiply and circulate copies of Livy, which is in a
real sense the Scripture of the Roman ideal. And it is as a

religious ideal that Rutilius Namatianus, the last of the
pagan poets, bids his farewell to Rome:

> You brought the nations one great fatherland,
> you raised the savage with your taming hand,
> broke him, but gave him laws to be his aid.
> A City of the scattered Earth you made.
>   (Translated by Jack Lindsay)

The City into which Rome had made the scattered Earth
continued as a City, and indeed the new unifying principle
was more exigent than the old had been. In its service men
continued to do what came into their hands to do, and did
it as well as they might. Perhaps the most telling change,
from the point of view of the present essay, is a new anonymity which took the place of assertive individuality. In the
classical age poets and sculptors had competed publicly for
the distinction of having their names recorded, and works of
literature or art were always referred to by the name of the
author. Quintilian or even a soldier like Velleius Paterculus
or a dozen others can list the names and merits of canonical
authors. The Elder Pliny does the same for the ancient succession of sculptors. In a later century Diogenes Laertius
lists the succession of philosophers, from the beginnings,
with their individual doctrines. Athenaeus in Greek and
Aulus Gellius in Latin fill their pages with literary gossip of
personages long dead. There was a long tradition of such
information and many systematic works, now lost, from
which these authors drew.

Certain works of high antiquity, early "geometric" pot-
tery, "Homeric" hymns, archaic "Apollos," are, for us,
anonymous, but they were probably not so for their con-

temporaries. The significant thing is that names were so often attached to works of unknown authorship. Thucydides, for example, knows that the hymn to Apollo, which cannot have been Homer's, is Homeric. Xenophon is praised by later writers for not claiming Thucydides' work as his own when he might have done so. Works of unknown authorship came to be associated, however improbably, with authors that were known: so the un-Platonic dialogues in the corpus of Plato, the treatise we attribute to the "Old Oligarch" in the corpus of Xenophon, the un-Plutarchan essays in the corpus of Plutarch, the *Appendix Vergiliana*. Any literate Greek could name the architects who designed the Parthenon and the sculptor who decorated it; the great medieval cathedrals are truly anonymous.

Rome naturally inherited the Greek concern for recording individual authorship. If we know no Roman sculptors it is because there were none to set beside the Greek masters. Rome considered the plastic arts banausic and the carvers and painters who worked in Rome were actually Greeks. But Roman writers were as insistent on their own fame as were the Greeks, and asserted proudly that they would not wholly die but continue through the ages, that they had builded themselves monuments more enduring than bronze. It is significant that a retired lawyer like Silius Italicus should wish to perpetuate his name by writing an epic poem. We see the conviction, resuscitated in the humanist age, that the greatest possible glory a man could win for himself was through authorship of an epic poem.

In the traditions of the east which affected Christianity the work was more important than the author. Anonymous authors did ascribe their works to an important figure like

Solomon—as in the case of Proverbs, Song of Songs, Ecclesiastes, Wisdom of Solomon—but themselves they effaced. The First Book of the Maccabees, which was written in Hebrew, is anonymous. The Second Book of Maccabees, which was written in Greek and according to the patterns of Hellenistic historiography, declares that it is an epitome of the work of Jason of Cyrene. The writers of the numerous apocalypses which were produced in the intertestamentary period regularly ascribed their work to some figure from remote antiquity.

The artists of the Middle Ages followed a similar anonymity. Manuscripts of Livy whose production was procured by Symmachus state that fact in colopha. Cassiodorus set the model for medieval scriptoria at Squillace, but the useful and sometimes artistic work of the scribes is anonymous. One of the most striking aspects of the Renaissance is the new concern to win individual renown for work done. Works of art as of literature are proudly signed, and we can see the precipitate of the obsession for individual recognition in the series of lives of George Vasari. There are, indeed, lives of saints also, but these are hagiographic works for edification, in direct succession to the ancient aretologies. A saint concerned for fame in his lifetime is a contradiction in terms.

The third channel is that of the Greeks themselves, continuous and not requiring to be reawakened in a renaissance. Preoccupation with development in the west has blinded all but a few students to the cultural history of Byzantium; the fact is that the ancient texts and the atmosphere they reflected were the central object of study in Byzantium all through its history. The object of education, from the child's earliest years was *hellenizein,* which meant to know the ancient language correctly, and the mark of the educated man was *hellenismos,* which referred to knowledge of the ancient language and literature. If the ancient tradition had entered into symbiosis with orthodox Christianity, it still remained a shared legacy and a symbol for humane discourse, and its values were understood and esteemed. The scholarly refugees from Constantinople in the sixteenth century were not exclusively responsible for the renaissance in the west, but they were certainly influential in it, and the sum of their influence was the ancient legacy which had been preserved and cultivated in the east during the preceding millennium.

IX.

Humanist Revival

WHAT the removal of Victory signified, if Rome's claim was also basically religious, was the substitution of a new overriding dominion for an old, and the transfer was easy and for people less sensitive than Symmachus scarcely perceptible. But the consequences for the outlooks and eventually conduct of men were profound, for the objects of religious devotion were fundamentally different. The object of Christians' loyalty was outside this world, in which they considered themselves only as sojourners. The object of pagan loyalty, as the apostrophe of Rutilius shows, was human achievement in this world. Service to the pagan ideal involved self-generated assertion of individuality and the personal reward of highly desirable fame among one's contemporaries and even posterity. Service to the Christian ideal implied the submergence of personality; the recognition of such service in the real and enduring other world reduced worldly fame to a meaningless and even contemptible bagatelle. The one encouraged assertion of individuality, the other produced anonymity. Originally neglect of the one code was merely a sign of fecklessness and violation merely a crime; violation of the other code was a grievous sin. But even before Constantine's edict made Christianity the state religion the imperial office had moved toward unqualified autocracy and its holders demanded religious adoration, but certain aspects of the old order remained, as a brief résumé will show.

The principate as originally designed, according to patterns drawn from the teachings of Posidonius and other masters of the Middle Stoa, provided that the ruler should possess extraordinary powers, but only as an administrator; the constitutional device employed was that the emperor held simultaneously and continuously certain key offices that were traditional in the republic. In any case it was clear that he must serve the state, not own it as an Oriental despot or even as the vicar of deity. It is true that certain of even the early emperors, the mad Caligula for example, insisted upon a divine status; but the more prudent ones, Claudius as we know from his letter to the Egyptians and of course Marcus Aurelius, pointedly refused to arrogate the prerogatives of divinity to themselves. The position, and the dangers to which it was susceptible, become clear from Seneca's addresses to his pupil Nero. Here is a typical passage from his *On Clemency* (19).

What could be more glorious than a life for whose wellbeing all offer prayer and all pronounce vows, with none to prod them? When an indisposition rouses men's fears, not their hopes? When nothing is so precious to an individual that he would not willingly exchange it for the health of his chief? Surely a man so fortunate owes it to himself to stay alive; the ever-present proofs of his goodness declare, not that the state belongs to him, but that he belongs to the state. Who would dare heap a stumbling block for such a king? Who would not elect to keep even accident away from a man under whom justice, peace, decency, security, and dignity flourish, under whom the state prospers and abounds in fullness of all good things? Men gaze upon their ruler with just such veneration and adoration as we should upon the immortal gods if they gave us the power of looking upon them. Actually, is he not nearest the gods when he comports himself in accordance with the nature of the gods and is beneficent and generous and potent for good? This should be your goal, this your pattern, to be held greatest only if you are at the same time best.

A change is indicated in a new definition of *laesa majestas,* which originally designated any offense against the state, and then came to designate any show of disrespect to the emperor. In a sense this is tantamount to conferring divinity upon the emperor, but the history of the usage makes it clear that the emperor claimed special consideration only as a symbol of the state. The more rational emperors and their rational subjects understood that the divinity claimed for the emperor meant only an authority to administer and to serve as a visible symbol of Rome. The circumstance that Rome had no ruling dynasty, so that new emperors attained adoption and succession by personal merit, helped to prevent the notion of divinity inhering in a blood line. Even in the fourth century the Emperor Julian and the orator Libanius objected to the concept of authority residing in the person of the ruler and sought to revert to the classical theory that all power is vested in the people, who only delegate it to the king.

The reaction under Julian shows that the man-centered conception still had strength, the failure of the reaction that it was doomed. The books which the reaction had cherished, and forbade Christian schools to use, were the classics— Sophocles, who had said in the famous first ode of the *Antigone,* "Wonders are many, but none is more wonderful than

man"; and Homer, whose young warriors were enjoined
always to strive for excellence and always to surpass all
others. When the reaction failed a new code became paramount: "Thou shalt worship the Lord thy God, and him
only shalt thou serve." This service required surrender
rather than self-assertion, anonymity rather than the fame
of the innovator.

It may be that after a millennium of strenuous and man-
centered self-assertion people subsided into anonymity and
other worldly expectations with a sense of relief. The old
world lapsed into the new, which was now without a rival.
Because the range of the new authority was so wide and its
seat so lofty, it could eventually brook assertion of individuality that was not directed against itself, and it may be
significant that the new heroes who approach (but do not
reach) Achilles' self-sufficiency derive from peoples outside
the old Greco-Roman orbit. Beowulf (whose author doubtless knew the *Aeneid*) falls short because he deals with
magic and because his suppression of Grendel and Grendel's
dam and the fire-drake is in the service of true religion. A
hero like Roland comes nearer. He can assert his prowess
and his pride almost with the freedom of an Achilles, but
not entirely, for there is an essential difference. Roland is a
vassal of God first and foremost, and his enterprise is on
behalf of Christendom and against the paynims. He and his
men have been assured by the Archbishop Turpin that their
doughty blows will win them eternal bliss, and at his death
Roland reaches his glove to the Archangel Michael, who
receives it. Here the sphere of the human and the divine are
so closely interwoven that they virtually coincide. If Roland's
code too is "To be always among the bravest and hold his

head above others," his doing so is in fulfillment of the commandment "Thou shalt worship the Lord thy God and Him only shalt thou serve." The Greeks and their pupils who kept the human and the divine apart served man.

But though the Greek view had been supplanted it was not wholly erased. It may be that even Roland's heroism is a distant echo. Vergil at least was read more or less continuously through the Middle Ages, perhaps only because the Fourth Eclogue was believed to prophesy the coming of Christ and Vergil himself was thought to be Christian. Dante, who knew him and his age well, revered him. The care with which notable persons, ancient and modern, are identified in the *Divine Comedy* is a mark of the new age. The pagan writers who appear in the *Divine Comedy* are not eligible for eternal bliss but they are highly esteemed nevertheless, and Dante himself assumes a place beside them. It is clear that authorship of a great poem is again the highest reach mortal man can attain, and if in the Purgatory they are nothing more than hoarse shadows, in the Renaissance they found their voices again and spoke loud and clear.

The Renaissance was neither as sudden, as spectacular, nor as revolutionary as it has frequently been painted. From the point of view of philosophy the distinctions from what had gone before were minor. All of the leading figures were believing and loyal Christians. Their principal innovation was to make large place for practical philosophy, the *ars bene beateque vivendi,* and though the shift of interest might eventually lead to theological doubts, to the men of the Renaissance it suggested what to us might seem an intensification of the religious view. They insisted strongly, for example, on the personal immortality of the soul, but they did so because personal immortality served as a banner in the struggle for more individualistic and personal values.

What the rebirth really meant was a fresh realization of man—his high achievements and higher potentialities, his independence and his self-sufficiency. The glorification of man was the favorite theme of early Renaissance literature, and concern with man is what gives its primary meaning to the word humanism. But the collateral meanings of the word, in common usage, are significant. The first of these is of course concern with the literature of classical antiquity, which is why we sometimes speak of the classics as *the* humanities. Whether humanism in the first sense is the cause or effect of humanism in the second is no great matter. The fact is that the humanists steeped themselves in the humanities until eventually not only their modes of writing and reasoning but their entire outlook was shaped to a substantial degree by the outlook of the ancients. Knowledge of and interest in some of the classics had never disappeared, as we can see from Dante, but now men took up where antiquity left off, with the intervening centuries telescoped. The humanists sought to make themselves at home in the climate of classical antiquity, and Greeks or Romans of the classic periods would surely have felt less alien in the climate of humanism than they would have done in the centuries that separated the two worlds.

On the lips of the devout, humanism has a third and pejorative meaning, as it inevitably must, for adding weight to one scale of the balances must inevitably lighten the other. Excessive concern with the human must militate against concern with the divine. The objections are precisely those adduced against the Sophists by their opponents in the fifth century B.C., and in both cases the opposition is well founded. It is of course possible to cite a long and imposing list of Christian humanists from Erasmus to this day; most Greeks too were at once humanist and observant of religious requirements. Perhaps the clearest example of the Christian humanist is Jerome Vida, whose *Christiad* is at once passionately devout and at the same time closer to the style and spirit of the *Aeneid* than any other Latin poem. Vida's verse treatise on poetics, his *Ars Poetica* (written about 1550), envisages the *Aeneid* as the supreme poetic model. At 3.186 f. in this treatise Vida prescribes—

adi monumenta priorum
crebra oculis, animoque legens, et multa voluta—

"Draw nigh the monuments of the ancients, scan them with your eyes, peruse them with your spirit, scrutinize them again and again." And for subject matter Vida prescribes, near the opening of his treatise, *post divos heroum facta recensent,* "Next after the gods, poets should chronicle the deeds of heroes." The divine, that is to say, is paramount but apart; heroes should be dealt with in their own terms.

If the issue be crystallized and primary loyalties and objectives and aspirations be made the criterion, there is no question that the institution of the city-state with all that it implied was the central factor for the preponderant number of classical Greeks, and no question that in this sense the national states of Europe which came into being after the Renaissance are the natural successors of the ancient city-states. The national state, like the ancient city-state, may foster religion and be supported by it, but the decisive aspect of its character is that it is itself a human institution. In all things its criterion is Protagoras': man is the measure. Because it is a human institution the state must unremittingly strive for higher excellence in its kind, as a true theocracy need not. Nor, where man is tacitly accepted as the measure, can the individuals who comprise the state remain static. They too must strive unremittingly to achieve ever higher excellence.

The key to the achievement of the classical Greeks is the constant striving for *aristeia* which was enjoined upon the heroes of Homer and which informed all Greek life. Nothing in the Greek legacy has been so effective in shaping European ways and outlooks. We are what we are because, however subconsciously, we too accept striving for *aristeia* as the code of conduct.

X.

The Return: Machiavelli and Spinoza

THE SPECIFICALLY Greek outlook proceeds from Homer onward like a broad highway, along an area covered also by secondary roads, and with tributaries debouching from or merging with the main road. Somewhere in the Roman period, to retain the image, secondary roads combined to cause a marked detour, which eventually, with Renaissance and humanism, gradually rejoined and merged with the main highway. Its character was inevitably altered, but in its outlines and direction it was unmistakably a continuation of the Greek way.

If we look at the authors of the sixteenth century who have an assured place in the general European cultural tradition we shall find that precisely that element which defines their quality and sets them apart from their predecessors is an ingredient characteristic of the Greek way. In all, to a greater or lesser degree, it is a renewal of the doctrine of man the measure. The ferment of the doctrine is to be discerned in all the writing of the age, scholarly as well as belletristic and religious as well as secular; it is most palpable, perhaps, in serious sketches of ideal polities such as are suggested by More (1478–1535), and Rabelais (1490–1553), and Montaigne (1533–1592).

Perhaps the most remarkable thing about More's *Utopia* is that its author, who himself suffered martyrdom for religion's sake, excluded from his ideal state preachers of

religion whose zeal was excessive. The entire organization
of Utopia is thoroughly secular. There is, to be sure, a
strong central administration, but its authority rests upon
the sovereignty of the people, not upon external or self-
willed powers, and its object is to provide for the highest
fulfillment of individuals. Such discipline and constraints
upon individual freedom as are prescribed, as for example
in the prohibition of private property, are in the nature of
police regulations, to prevent exploitation of the weak or indifferent by the strong and ambitious. War too is a police
matter, not a noble adventure. The state's main object in
accumulating wealth is to be able to bribe enemy leaders or
procure their assassination. Education is paramount, and
directed toward deepening and liberating individuality. To
this end degrading tasks like butchering are performed by
outsiders, and provision is made for recognition of excellence in intellectual and artistic endeavor. In none of the
regulations is there any thought of following a divinely
prescribed pattern or recovering a blessed state from which
mankind has degenerated.

Rabelais reposes so complete a trust in individual man
that even the police function virtually disappears. The motto
for the ideal society which he sketches in the Abbey of
Thélème is "Do what thou wilt," and at every point the
rigid prescriptions of the ordinary abbey, which are calculated to prevent a man from doing what he naturally would,
are systematically nullified. Where ordinary abbeys are dank
and forbidding, Thélème is sunny and attractive. The rigid
schedule of hours is totally abolished, for clocks are banished
from the Abbey. Instead of drab and uniform habits, dress
is colorful and elegant and varied, and instead of strict

segregation of sexes men and women are encouraged to associate freely. Where the system represented by ordinary abbeys premises the natural depravity of man, who can rise only by strenuous and directed efforts, the Abbey of Thélème is premised upon the natural goodness of man, in whom corruption is caused by the constraints of the world about him. If the causes of distortion are eliminated and the nature of man is allowed to assert itself freely, it will bloom and attain its proper excellence. Because Thélème is so obviously a denial of what had gone before it is clearer here than in the case of More's Utopia that the underlying rationale is the Greek doctrine of man the measure.

Montaigne's imaginary polity, located like More's in a newly discovered western island, is described in his essay *On Cannibals*. The usages in this polity are indeed different from those current in Europe, but Montaigne warns us that "there is nothing in that nation that is either barbarous or savage, unless men call that barbarisme which is not common to them. As indeed, we have no other Ayme of truth and reason, than the example and Idea of the opinions and customes of the countrie we live in." This is precisely the object of the Sophists' distinction between *physis* and *nomos*. The islanders are to be judged only on the basis of *physis*, by which criterion their usages are admirable, not by an alien *nomos*. "Those that gull and conicatch us with the assurance of an extraordinairie facultie, and which is beyond our knowledge, ought to be doubly punished." The cannibals do have discipline and bring their young up to their ideals by education, but the object of their discipline is to develop a high sense of individual worth and responsibility. To this end they cultivate equality; "they have a manner of

phrase whereby they call men but a moytie one of another."
It is the unnatural class stratification of Europeans which
most astonishes Montaigne's informants. "They had perceived that there were men amongst us full gorged with all
sortes of commodities, and other which hunger-starved and
bare with need and povertie, begged at their gates: and
found it strange, these moyties so needy could endure such
an injustice, and that they tooke not the others by the throte,
or set fire on their houses." Again at the close of his essay
Montaigne underscores the distinction of *nomos* and *physis;*
after detailing praises of the cannibals, he writes: "All that
is not verie ill; but what of that? They weare no kinde of
breeches nor hosen."

In all these utopias the common denominator is the en-
hanced importance and hence independence of the individual, of which the inevitable concomitant is the reduced
authority of external sanctions, governmental or religious.
Actually, in the last analysis, it is the secular authority of
organized religion that is put into question, for from the
time of the Roman Empire onward government had more
and more based its authority upon religious sanctions. None
of the three writers mentioned was an apostate from religion; all observed their Christian duties. The direction of
their efforts was, in effect, to keep the divine and human
spheres apart, as the Greeks had kept them apart, and so
to release man to achieve the highest human excellence of
which he is capable.

Separately or in combination, government and organized
religion are the factors which control the lives of men. The
first step in making man rather than external authority the
measure of all things is to separate government from re-

ligion, and this was done, most explicitly and thoroughly, by
Machiavelli (1469–1527). The second step is to separate religion from an organized authority based on a specific revelation, and this was done, most explicitly and thoroughly,
by Spinoza (1632–1677). In a real sense, therefore, these
two mark the principal stages in the return from the long
detour to the main road whose character and direction were
determined by the Greeks. We must glance at the work of
these men to see how this may be so.

Machiavelli's *Realpolitik* is too notorious to require com-
ment. All the resources that a prince, actual or intending,
can count upon to win or retain rule are those within
himself; he is answerable to no external power or code of
conduct, nor does he claim, except as a device to secure
discipline, that he rules by the grace of God. The heart of
the matter is in the fifteenth chapter of the *Prince,* entitled
"The Way Princes Should Keep Faith": "It is unnecessary
for a prince to have all the good qualities I have enumer-
ated, but it is very necessary to appear to have them. And
I shall dare to say this also, that to have them and always
observe them is injurious, and that to appear to have them
is useful; to appear merciful, faithful, humane, religious,
upright, and to be so, but with a mind so framed that should
you require not to be so, you may be able and know how
to change to the opposite."

Machiavellianism had always been practiced by successful princes, as Machiavelli's own pages show, but not since
the Athenians at Melos and Thrasymachus in the first book
of the *Republic* had the unqualified principle that might
makes right been proclaimed so starkly. After Machiavelli
as before him there have always been intelligent men who

understood that government entails Machiavellianism; what has outraged Machiavelli's readers and made them call him Old Nick is the factual tone of his book: he should at least have deplored human depravity and urged reform. Nevertheless, Machiavelli has served as a guide, consciously or otherwise, in the governments of Europe.

Sensitive readers have found Machiavelli's *Discourses on the First Decade of Livy* more sympathetic than his *Prince* because the *Discourses* deal with a republican rather than a princely form of government and show greater concern for the welfare of individuals. But in fact the *Discourses* show that Machiavellianism is as essential for a republic as for a principality. The *Discourses* praise or blame the heroes of republican Rome according as they weakened or strengthened the discipline of the state, and apply no other criterion; and their most effective and therefore most admirable means for securing discipline was their shrewd exploitation of religion. Here it is interesting to observe that Machiavelli goes behind the patriotic Livy to the pragmatic Polybius. Livy and Scipio himself, for example, apparently believed that Scipio was in fact vouchsafed special communications when he retired into the temple of Jupiter; Polybius had praised Scipio by insisting that he himself held no such belief but was clever enough to exploit a popular superstition for political ends. A significant passage in Polybius (6.56.9) will show how directly Machiavelli takes up where the Greeks had left off:

My own opinion at least is that the Romans have adopted this course of propagating religious awe for the sake of the common people. It is a course which perhaps would not have been necessary had it been possible to form a state composed of wise men, but as every multitude is fickle, full of lawless desires, unreasoned passion, and violent anger, the multitude must be held in by invisible terrors and suchlike pageantry. For this reason, I think, not that the ancients acted rashly and at haphazard in introducing among the people notions concerning the gods and beliefs in the terrors of hell, but that the moderns are most rash and foolish in banishing such beliefs.

Even Moses, whom Machiavelli brackets with Theseus as prudent and successful founders of enduring polities, is considered mainly as ruler, not as prophet, though his stature as prophet is in no way diminished. The point is that the realm of government had become independent of the realm of religion.

In government, then, the separateness of the human and divine spheres is recognized, and the return to the doctrine of man the measure is complete. Actually, when an author like Machiavelli suggests that religion may be manipulated for government's sake, the plain implication is that in religion too man is the measure. Within its own sphere, however, the validity of religion based on authorized interpretation of divine revelation was not questioned by such authors as we have glanced at, though, if only by implication, they do criticize the abuses within the religious system and the excessive extension of its authority. Even when such criticism reached the point of denying the legitimacy of the religious authority as then organized, divine revelation remained the charter on which religion was based. Unless a man refused to recognize religion and withdrew from it, he acknowledged the validity of the charter however much he might impugn special interpretations of it.

The final step of achieving what must be called (though surely not in any orthodox sense) a religious outlook based not on revelation but on human reason, as Euclid's geometry is based on human reason, was taken by Spinoza. Like the pre-Socratics or the Sophists or the Epicureans, Spinoza's ultimate and utter reliance is on the powers of the human mind. If philosophy is defined as a wholly independent quest of the human mind, then as Professor Wolfson has insisted, there is no philosophy between Philo of Alexandria and Spinoza. There were subtle and ingenious and devoted thinkers in the interval between the two, Christian and Jewish and Muslim, but all premised a pre-existing truth which required no seeking and admitted no questioning, so that what was left for the human intellect was in effect to reconcile other paths to truth with the paramount truth of revelation. What is important about Spinoza's enterprise, in the present context, is not the soundness or acceptability of his demonstration but the fact that he insisted on geometrical procedures, not on revelation or tradition, to prove the being and nature of the divine.

Put in the grossest terms, the salient difference between the God of the Christian-Jewish-Muslim philosophers and Spinoza's God is that Spinoza's God is not preoccupied with the affairs and destiny of man, that "all final causes are nothing but human fictions." "Men consider all things as made for themselves," he writes in the Appendix to the first book of his *Ethics,* "and call the nature of a thing good, evil, sound, putrid, or corrupt just as they are affected by it." And since man has assumed that "the gods direct everything for his advantage," for the workings of nature which do not obviously correspond to his interests he must "at last fly to the will of God—the refuge of ignorance."

Confident assertion concerning the divine shaped by considerations of human interests according to human criteria is the thing that Homer and Sophocles and the Sophists objected to, the thing that Epicurus and Lucretius inveighed against. Spinoza is more systematic in his objections because he emerges from a world in which the other view had so long prevailed. His advocacy of the older view is conscious and calculated. He uses geometrical modes and Latin (which was the nearest approach to the language of mathematics) in order to eliminate the dangerous factors of imagination and emotion; actually his system presupposes an enormous imaginative sweep, and there is emotional zeal in his engagement with great issues and his concern for human freedom. Quite literally, Spinoza resumes the main line of what is peculiar to the Greek outlook just where Philo had diverted it.

In the post-Renaissance picture as a whole, Spinoza of course is rather a symptom than a cause of the return. But innovators in the centuries after Spinoza have similarly been symptoms. The three men who are usually reckoned catalysts for the most far-reaching changes in our modern outlooks are Darwin and Marx and Freud, and all three take up from a point where Greeks left off. The common denominator in all is a thoroughly anthropocentric point of departure and goal in an area where other gauges had been traditional. Darwin makes precise the adumbrations of the Epicurean Lucretius in regard to the development of animal creation. Marx systematizes Lucretius' theories of the origin of society and argues for the disinherited against constraints of convention as the Sophists had done, and with the anti-religious religiosity of the Epicureans. Freud proceeds from the premises of Greek tragedy, so that drama after Freud is essentially more like the Greek than antecedent post-classical drama has been. Both the classic and the modern are premised not so much, as the usual definition of tragedy has it, on tensions between a man and an external fate, but on the ego and id in man. In both external fate is a thing apart; the spheres of the human and the divine are disparate.

But aside from innovations which may be considered advances along paths laid down by the Greeks, the motive impulse which impelled men to achieve them, indeed the motive impulse which makes European culture, in contrast with others, a restless striving for innovation in every direction, which makes public notice so desirable a goal, which impels men to spend themselves in striving to surpass others —that impulse is itself Greek, and perhaps the central and all-subsuming factor in our Greek legacy.

In a hundred lesser ways that legacy had persisted through the earlier history of Europe, and indeed in many ways continuity with the old was more apparent before the humanist age than after it. But though the modern world seems to have made a sharper break with the old, actually it is a more direct continuation of the remoter than of the nearer path. The long detour has fed back into the main highway, and man is again invited to push forward the horizons of the humanly possible and encouraged to strive for the highest excellence of which man himself is capable.